NATIONAL FOUNDATION FOR EDUCATIONAL
RESEARCH IN ENGLAND AND WALES
RESEARCH REPORTS. SECOND SERIES, No. 5

TEACHING BEGINNERS TO READ

REPORT No. 2

Teachers and their
Pupils' Home Background

A

Teachers and their Pupils' Home Background

An Investigation into Teachers' Attitudes
and Expectations in Relation to their Estimates and Records of Pupils' Abilities,
Attributes and Reading Attainment

by

E. J. GOODACRE, B.Sc.(Econ.), Ph.D.

NATIONAL FOUNDATION FOR EDUCATIONAL
RESEARCH IN ENGLAND AND WALES
THE MERE, UPTON PARK, SLOUGH, BUCKS

Published by the National Foundation for Educational Research
in England and Wales

The Mere, Upton Park, Slough, Bucks
and at 79 Wimpole Street, London, W.1

First Published 1968

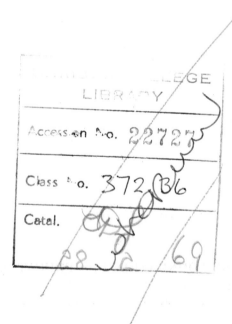

Printed in Great Britain by
KING, THORNE & STACE LTD., SCHOOL ROAD, HOVE   BN3 5JE

Preface

DURING the months which have elapsed since the publication of the first report of this research, *Reading in Infant Classes*, many readers will have given some time to the study of the Plowden Report[1] and to another recent publication, *11,000 Seven-Year-Olds*.[2]

Thus there is little need to stress again the critical importance of the nursery and infant years of education, the need to take account of children's home background and to reconsider the arrangements for the admission of children to different stages of primary education.

In her second report, Dr. Goodacre presents a detailed study of the nature of teachers' attitudes and background—professional and otherwise—and considers the possible influences of these on the progress of infants learning to read, and the estimates which teachers make of this progress. She has included an interesting analysis of teachers' concepts of reading readiness.

The analysis of the children's attainments in terms of the nature of the area from which they come, confirms and illuminates the suggestion that the factor of social class is far more complex in its influence that most of us have yet fully realized.

Perhaps the most interesting result emerging from this second report is the suggestion that the professional practice of infant teachers may be in part induced by stereotypes and expectations which are only partially true. This leads to the even more pertinent question of how such expectations affect teaching, a question which has yet to be fully examined.

[1] CENTRAL ADVISORY COUNCIL FOR EDUCATION (ENGLAND) (1967). *Children and their Primary Schools*. A report of the Central Advisory Council for Education (England). Vol. 1: The Report; Vol. 2: Research and Surveys. London: H.M. Stationery Office.
[2] PRINGLE, M. L. K. *et al.* (1966). *11,000 Seven-Year-Olds*. First Report of the National Child Development Study (1958 Cohort) submitted to the Central Advisory Council for Education (England). London: Longmans.

Preface

As with so much that is good in the growing field of educational research, this work has involved very wide collaboration. The NFER would like to place on record its debt to the London County Council Education Committee for their permission to undertake our research programme in the infant schools and departments under their authority and for their continued assistance, to the very many Education Officers, Inspectors, heads and class teachers who not only collaborated in the onerous field work, but who willingly consulted with us at all the stages of planning and conduct of the inquiry; and to Miss E. M. Puddephat, Dr. D. F. Swift and Dr. J. C. Daniels for reading and commenting on the manuscript.

We are, of course, specially indebted to Dr. Goodacre herself. Most of the field work of this and the previous inquiry was completed whilst she was in the service of the NFER; and most of the statistical work was done under the general supervision of Miss Jill Tarryer, by the Foundation's Data Processing and Statistical Services. The writing of the report had to be carried through by Dr. Goodacre in the interstices of the life of a busy mother of young children. In the later stages of the preparation of the report, she was helped by my colleague Mr. Brian Cane and by Mrs. Amy Brown who assisted in the work of final revision.

W. D. WALL

December 1967

iv

Author's Acknowledgements

Dr. Wall has mentioned already the many people to whom I am indebted for their detailed work on different aspects of this book, and in endorsing his thanks I should like to mention particularly the helpfulness of the heads, staffs and pupils of the London schools, whose patient and generous assistance in providing information made this research possible.

Also, I would like to acknowledge the guidance and encouragement which I received at various stages of the research from Dr. Wall himself, Mr. D. A. Pidgeon, Dr. Joyce Morris, Dr. K. M. Miller, and Professor Hilda Himmelweit who as my tutor steered me through my higher degree studies, and like those previously mentioned, clarified many aspects of the work with perceptive criticism.

E. J. GOODACRE

December 1967

Contents

page

PREFACE iii

AUTHOR'S ACKNOWLEDGEMENTS   v

LIST OF TABLES   viii

INTRODUCTION.   Origins and Scope of the Report   .. xi

I.   Survey of Previous Research   1

II.   Sources of Information 9

Note: Statistical and Educational Significance   14

III.   The Main Findings   15

IV.   Pupils' Home Background   26

V.   Assessments of Individual Pupils   48

VI.   Teachers' Attitudes and Personalities 58

VII.   A Note on Future Research   73

APPENDICES

   A.   Selection of Schools   77

   B.   Questionnaires and Forms   79

   C.   Additional Information, Chapter II 121

   D.   Additional Information, Chapter IV 127

   E.   Additional Information, Chapter V 141

   F.   Additional Information, Chapter VI 151

   G.   Bibliography   165

INDEX   169

List of Tables

page

IV/A   Mean Rating by All Teachers (N=275) of Items Describing the 'Good' Home   31

IV/B   Intercorrelations of Three Assessments of Pupils' Social Class—(1) Teachers' Estimates, (2) Social Class Index Based on Census Data, (3) Pupils' Recorded Paternal Occupations   42

V/A   Teachers' Knowledge of Individual Pupils' Home Background   49

V/B   Percentage of Children Attaining Each Reading Readiness Characteristic (First and Second Years)   55

APPENDIX C

C/I   Numbers of Schools, Teachers and Children completing the Various Instruments from the Reading Inquiry which were used in the Study of Teachers' Attitudes   122

C/II   Social Areas and Social Class Indices   123

C/III   Comparison of London 1960-61 and National Survey Figures 1955 of London Infant Women Teachers' and Primary Women Teachers' Social Class Origins   125

C/IV   Distribution of Schools (by Organization and Social Area) and Teachers (by Staff Position and Social Class Origin) completing each part of the Teachers' Attitude Study   126

APPENDIX D

D/I   Characteristics of a 'Good' Home   128

D/II   Characteristics of a 'Poor' Home   129

D/III   Characteristics of a 'Good' Home: Comparison of Importance Based on Content Analysis (N=208 teachers) and Rating (N=275 teachers)   130

D/IV   Home Background (General) Form: Means for Sub-scores of Teachers in Different School Organizations (N=275 teachers)   131

D/V   Home Background (General) Form: Means for the Sub-scores of Teachers in Different Age Groups (N=137 teachers)   133

D/VI	Home Background (General) Form: Mean Total Scores for Different Groups of Teachers	134
D/VII	Intercorrelations of Five Social Variables and Teachers' Social Class Origin	136
D/VIII	(a) Intercorrelations of Heads' Over/Under Estimation of Pupils' Social Class and their Estimates of Pupils' Intelligence and Parental Interest	139
	(b) Intercorrelations of Heads' Social Class Origin and Estimates of Pupils' Intelligence and Parental Interest	139

APPENDIX E

E/I	Organization Differences within Social Areas for Teachers' Estimates of Individual Pupils' Home Background	143
E/II	Teachers' Estimates of Individual Pupils in Relation to Six Factors Relevant to Pupils' Reading Achievement	144
E/III	Pupils' Achieved Book Levels (six point scale)	149
E/IV	Pupils' Reading Progress (three point scale)	149
E/V	Predictions of Pupils' Success (three point scale)	150

APPENDIX F

F/I	Age Distribution of Total and Groups of Teachers	151
F/II	Marital Status Distribution for Total and Groups of Teachers	152
F/III	Place of Birth for Total and Groups of Teachers	152
F/IV	Length of Teaching Service for Total and Groups of Teachers	153
F/V	Length of Service in Present Post for Total and Groups of Teachers	153
F/VI	Infant Teachers' Strong and Weak Personality Traits	154
F/VII	Infant Teachers' Satisfactions and Dissatisfactions with Teaching	155
F/VIII	Intercorrelation Matrix for 94 Women Infant Teachers on 11 Variables	161
F/IX	Correlations between Head's Authoritarianism and Pupils' Reading Attainment	164
F/X	Correlations between Head's Attitude to Pupils' Home Background and Pupils' Reading Attainment	164

Introduction

THIS study of teachers' attitudes towards their pupils' home background and their expectations and assessments of individual pupils was designed as part of a larger, three-stage project concerned with the teaching of reading in infant schools. The project was initiated by the National Foundation for Educational Research in September 1958, and was carried out with the assistance of the London County Council Education Committee and Officers, the Ministry of Education Inspectorate and the Child Development Department of the University of London Institute of Education.

The main aims of the three-year inquiry were (1) to investigate the nature and extent of the task of teaching infants to read, particularly in schools in areas where little assistance could be expected from children's homes, and (2) to study the reading readiness, attainment and progress of the children in relation to their individual attributes, home circumstances and school conditions.

The results of the first stage of the investigation—a survey of methods, materials, conditions and pupils' achievements in 100 schools and departments—were published early in 1967.[1] One of the most interesting aspects of the findings given in the first report was the difference between the teachers' evaluations of the children's reading ability and the children's tested performance. The teachers' assessments (based on their records of book level reached) indicated that children in middle and upper working-class areas showed markedly superior reading ability in comparison with children in lower working-class areas, with the middle-class pupils showing superior attainment. However, the superiority of middle-class pupils was not found when pupils' reading attainments were tested by means of standardized reading comprehension group tests. The working-class pupils appeared to do better than might have been expected, especially in relation to tested attainment, but the lower

[1] GOODACRE, E. J. (1967). *Reading in Infant Classes.* Report No. 1: Teaching Beginners to Read. Slough: NFER.

xi

working-class pupils were markedly inferior in comparison with the other two groups, whichever criteria was used—estimated or tested reading attainment.

The fact that the upper working-class pupils did better than might have been anticipated, particularly in relation to the more objective criteria (scores on a standardized test) suggested that factors other than teaching methods and school conditions might affect the level of pupils' reading attainment. One such factor might be the teachers' expectations of their pupils' abilities and attainment. These expectations might also serve to explain the difference between pupils' tested and assessed attainments; and it is possible that, in fact, teachers' assessments reflect the standards they apply to pupils from particular social environments.

It is, of course, obvious that teachers do formulate opinions about their pupils' home backgrounds, and that their attitudes towards pupils—either as groups or as individuals—will affect in some way their teaching methods and their expectations as to the pupils' attainments. Since this project was initiated, there have been signs of an increasing awareness of the effects of home background and parental attitudes upon children's educational attainments. The evidence collected for the first report in this series indicated the possibility that the teachers' assessments of pupils' attainments might be affected by these attitudes, and there is also evidence from other sources (see Chapter I) that teachers' attitudes, as well as the pupils' self-evaluation, influence the behaviour of their pupils in the classroom.

Additional evidence of the influence of pupils' home background on pupils' attainment has been included in the Plowden Report,[1] together with a number of recommendations aimed at securing better co-operation between the teacher and the parent. As yet, however, there has been very little study of the process by which teachers become aware of differences in parental attitudes and formulate their opinions about home influences.

It is, therefore, important to discover not only how teachers' attitudes affect their actions, but how they come to formulate them and in what circumstances. This raises a multiplicity of questions. What, for instance, are the standards the teachers apply to different types of pupils? What are they really referring to when they talk

---

[1] DEPARTMENT OF EDUCATION AND SCIENCE: CENTRAL ADVISORY COUNCIL FOR EDUCATION (ENGLAND). (1967). *Children and their Primary Schools.* (Plowden Report). London: H.M. Stationery Office.

about 'good' and 'poor' homes? This report attempts to examine the following questions in relation to infants in a cross-section of schools in an urban setting:

1. What importance do infant teachers attach to pupils' home background in the teaching of reading?
2. How do teachers categorize pupils in relation to their home background?
3. What is the extent of teachers' personal contacts with pupils and their homes and what clues do they use as a basis for their impressions of pupils' home conditions?
4. If paternal occupation is used as a criterion for assessing pupils' home background, how reliable are teachers as judges'?
5. What inferences do teachers make about pupils whose parents follow different types of occupation?
6. To what extent do such inferences affect teachers' ratings of individual pupils?
7. Do teachers of infants have certain social and psychological characteristics, distinguishing them from teachers of older children in the educational system, which would be of importance in considering teachers' attitudes to pupils and their homes?
8. How far are differences in teachers' attitudes to pupils' home backgrounds related to psychological rather than sociological factors?
9. Do the personality and attitudes of the head have any direct bearing on the level of pupils' reading attainment?
10. In considering the process by which teachers formulate opinions about pupils' home background, how important are factors such as (a) the type of organization of the school in which the teacher works, (b) the teacher's position in the school, or (c) the teacher's own social class origin?

Plan of the report

Chapter I outlines the previous research which provides a background to the study, and Chapter II describes the procedure adopted in carrying it out and the type of material used. A note explaining statistical and educational significance precedes Chapter III, which summarizes the main findings. Chapters IV, V and VI deal with these findings in more detail—differences in relation to the school and teacher variables (school organization and social area; teacher position and social class origin) being reported where applicable. The report concludes with a note on future research.

It is hoped that the subject of the report will be of interest to those concerned with the practical difficulties involved in teaching young children to read, if only to encourage them to reconsider the generally accepted ideas about the influence of the home and to be more conscious of the implicit assumptions behind many of their teaching decisions.

Perhaps the report's most important contribution may be in relation to the research into the role of the teacher in remediation of learning disabilities among those pupils termed 'disadvantaged'. Certainly the teacher plays an important role in the life of pupils, but *what* it is and *how* it compensates for the disadvantages experienced by such pupils, is not clear. Further research on this aspect of education is clearly needed.

References

DEPARTMENT OF EDUCATION AND SCIENCE: CENTRAL ADVISORY COUNCIL FOR EDUCATION (ENGLAND). (1967). *Children and their Primary Schools.* (Plowden Report). London: H.M. Stationery Office.
GOODACRE, E. J. (1967). *Reading in Infant Classes.* Slough: NFER.

CHAPTER I

Survey of Previous Research

THE work of Sir Cyril Burt (1937) and the evidence of social surveys such as those of Merseyside (1934) and Middlesbrough (1948) indicated that low levels of educational attainment and backwardness were associated with the gross factors of poverty, poor housing and malnutrition. Since the war, however, social planning and the emergence of the welfare state have lessened the formerly more obvious material differences between the living conditions of different social groups, and recent studies have concentrated upon the more subtle reasons for differences in educational attainment such as attitudes, values and aspirations. [*Early Leaving* (1954); Floud, Halsey and Martin (1956); Fraser (1959); Douglas (1964); Wiseman (1964); Swift (1967); *Children and their Primary Schools* (1967).]

This emphasis on sociological factors has also been apparent in the research into the effectiveness of teachers. Although a considerable amount of evidence has been included on the selection, assessment and personality of teachers [Evans (1959a, 1959b), Allen (1962)], much of it has been inconclusive, and as Evans (1966) has suggested, teaching success has seemed to depend quite as much on 'the school situation in which a teacher finds himself as on his own qualities'. Inability to arrive at a consensus of opinion regarding the characteristics of the effective teacher, has encouraged researchers to concentrate on two particular aspects: (a) the role and function of the teacher and the way in which differences in the teacher's behaviour may be related to social pressures; and (b) the effectiveness of training procedures in altering or manipulating students' attitudes towards education.

Probably the most detailed explanation of the teacher's job in terms of role analysis is that produced by Blyth (1965). He has defined various aspects of the teacher's role in relation to the primary school, thereby clarifying the arguments put forward by Mays (1962) for broadening its scope, and by Floud (1962) for a reconsideration of the 'ideal' type of teacher needed if the teacher's function is to be brought into line with the needs and structure of our present democratic and affluent society. Briefly, Blyth has suggested that society ascribes to the teacher at least three types of role: the *classifier*, the *instructor* and the *socializer*. The teacher is expected to instruct pupils in the skills and techniques required by the stage of development of their society, and to do this it is necessary to assess pupils' abilities and aptitudes so as to be able to supply the appropriate level of instruction and guidance. The teacher prepares pupils to learn to work together in society, and Blyth distinguishes three aspects of this socializing function of the teacher, describing how the teacher acts (1) as a parent-substitute, initiating the child into the processes of society; (2) as an organizer, producing that degree of order in the classroom which makes learning in a group feasible, and (3) as a 'value-bearer', in the sense that he transmits those values and ideals which are associated with the larger unit of society and which distinguished its standards from the idiosyncratic ones of the family.

How different groups in society perceive the teacher's role and the ways in which different social environments affect the teacher's ability to carry out the various functions, are now beginning to be systematically explored. Musgrove (1961) studied parents' expectations of what they thought the junior school should provide and reported differences in relation to the social class of the parents— for example, working-class parents entrusted the teachers with greater responsibility for the behaviour-training of their children and expected them to encourage pupils to conform to authority, and not to challenge it. Webb (1962) stressed the importance of the organizing aspect of the socializer role which the secondary modern teacher assumed in lower working-class areas, vividly describing how the problems of maintaining authority could affect the other roles of instructor and classifier. Taylor (1962) obtained junior and secondary pupils' ratings of the characteristics of the 'good' teacher, and found that whereas pupils placed most emphasis on the teacher's ability to instruct, teachers and students evaluated most highly the 'good' teacher's personal qualities—those which produced behaviour approximating to that associated with the 'ideal' as presented by educationists, training college tutors, etc. Taylor concluded that pupils probably perceived the 'good' teacher's teaching as 'a means to the satisfaction of a need they have in our society: to be taught and to learn'. Rudd and Wiseman (1962) examined teachers' sources of dissatisfaction about their work, and concluded that sex differences were important. They suggested that women were more pre-occupied with day-to-day classroom problems, whilst men concentrated on external factors such as poor salaries and their professional status—factors which reflect society's evaluation of their role.

A detailed, thoughtful analysis of the teacher's role has been provided by Wilson (1962). This analysis, concentrating upon a sociological approach, has become a reference point for a number of researchers working in this aspect of the field. One of many points brought out was the fact that the teacher's role can be a source of anxiety to him because of the lack of overt criteria by which the teacher can judge the success of the performance of his role. The diffuseness of the role makes it difficult not only for the profession of teaching to win social approval, as evidenced by questions of prestige, salary, etc. but also implies, for the individual, diffuse involvement, creating problems of how to deal with guilt over 'not doing enough' and leading to tendencies to 'live with the job'.

Musgrove and Taylor (1965) compared parents' and teachers' expectations, and found evidence that while both groups tended to stress the instructional and socializing roles of the teacher, neither acknowledged the classifying role. This suggests that, at the present time, neither teachers nor parents have yet accepted the implications of certain recent developments in educational research, such as, for example, the denial of the constancy of the IQ. It appears that although teachers are increasingly becoming the agents of social advancement, both parents and teachers seem loath to recognize the fact. Finlayson and Cohen (1967) compared the views of heads and students in regard to the scope and nature of the teacher's role, and reported widespread disparity of opinion between the two groups. Practising teachers and heads showed most concern about the organizing aspect of the socializing role—the ability to produce the conditions in the classroom which facilitate the teacher's other functions. Cohen (1967) identified and compared the expectations held by students, tutors, experienced teachers and heads in relation to that aspect of the teacher's role concerned with liaison between home and school. He found that the idea of a more diffuse role for the teacher with closer contacts between home and school, received little support from heads, who tended rather to emphasize the

3

traditional approach to the role. This is characterized by the idea that a certain degree of social conformity must be accepted by a class before formal instruction becomes possible—whether in the skills or 'right' attitudes to work.

At this stage of summarizing the previous research, it is possible to relate the developments outlined to those which have occurred in the research on teacher effectiveness. The study by Finlayson and Cohen (1967), referred to above, reported that students' attitudes reached a peak of growing insight into the teacher's role in their second year of training but their ideas become more traditional as entry into the reality of the classroom became imminent, suggesting that college training indicated the 'ideal' towards which teachers should aspire but that in the real-life situation of the classroom, the practicalities of achieving order and control assumed more importance. Also it was probable that too great a difference between the 'role' conception of the newly appointed teacher and that of the head, would be bound to lead to considerable role conflict for the former. However, one other fact worth noting in this research is that there were large variances reported in all groups for many of the items involved, particularly in regard to actual behaviour in the classroom. It seems likely that personality factors may be important in relation to the extent to which a teacher's classroom behaviour is affected by these role expectations.

Certainly the main findings of the research on students' attitudes to education have centred round the identification of several major dimensions of personality (e.g. tendermindedness, authoritarianism, and progressiveness or radicalism), and that although students' attitudes do change during training, the tendency is for their attitudes to become less progressive and more traditional once they are inside the schools. At this stage of research, it is difficult to differentiate between the effects of age and of experience in the schools. [Koch, *et al.* (1934); Harding (1944a, b); Kerlinger and Kaya (1959a, b); Oliver and Butcher (1962); Butcher (1965); Tuppin (1966); Horn and Morrison (1965); Evans (1966); McIntyre, *et al.* (1966); McIntyre and Morrison (1967).]

One of the main prerequisites of effective teaching is the ability to impose order and meaning on the complex environment of the classroom. As part of the organizing process, teachers will classify

4

and label their pupils.[1]   Hallworth has provided some information about how teachers judge pupils, in a series of reports on teachers' ratings of pupils' personalities (1961, 1962, 1965); with Morrison (1964).   According to Hallworth it appeared that teachers were judging their pupils largely in terms of two dimensions of meaning— 'emotional stability' and 'social extra-version'—as applied within the context of school life.   'An assessment of a boy's emotional stability or conscientiousness and reliability was in fact a measure of the teacher's general attitude to him as a pupil.   Similarly, an assessment of his social extra-version was the teacher's assessment of his activity within the social life of the school'.   It is as if the teacher were asking himself; first, 'How much do I approve of this boy or girl as a *pupil*?'; and, secondly, 'How active is he or she in the group life of the class, and to what extent will they influence the group and therefore help or hinder my intentions?'   Hallworth has suggested that these dimensions of personality discernible in the teacher's rating are typical of those which may be obtained from any situation in which judgements are made of either adults or children (e.g. Eysenck's work, 1953), and that they indicate two very simple but common means of classifying and describing people.

This line of approach was developed further by McIntyre, Morrison and Sutherland (1965, 1966), who examined teachers' assessments of pupils' personality traits and attainment, and reported (a) that there were three major dimensions (in positive terms): 'good behaviour', 'high attainment' and 'sociability and social leadership'; (b) that, in general, teachers' assessments of physical maturation, and objective measurements of attendance/absenteeism and sociometric status were independent of other traits; and (c) that teachers tended to make more general evaluations of girls than boys.   When the data was analysed according to the social-class background of

---

[1] The way in which teachers organize their classrooms will influence their pupils, producing certain types of behaviour.   Lewin, Lippitt and White (1939), in an artificial situation, demonstrated the effect on pupils' behaviour of different types of leadership patterns.   However, physical conditions may bring about a change of behaviour in the teacher, e.g. Anderson and Brewer (1945-6) reported that 'dominative' behaviour on the part of the teacher increased in the afternoons and as the term went on'.   One must also keep in mind the fact that pupils will have been prepared by their families to expect a particular type of leadership from the teacher; for example, Jones (1966) states that working-class children were prepared by their mothers for a passive role in school.   In any particular situation, it is difficult to predict which will occur: that teachers will consciously adopt certain behaviour, because it fits in with pupils' expectations or that they will expect pupils to change their attitudes.   The age, experience and personality of the teacher as well as the personality and family background of individual pupils are all likely to be influential factors.

the school, age and experience of the teacher, and the teachers' opinions about education, some interesting results emerged. Teachers' assessments were made in terms of two main dimensions, but the traits defining these dimensions differed according to the social class of the pupils, their sex, and the age and experience of the teachers. For instance, the assessments of the younger teachers stressed good behaviour, whereas the older teachers placed greater emphasis on high attainment and such associated 'work' traits as persistance and enthusiasm, suggesting that they were more assured about handling classes than were the younger teachers with less experience. When asked for their views regarding the 'pupil worth taking trouble over', teachers in middle-class and mixed social-class schools laid stress on traits descriptive of the 'pleasant' and 'trust-worthy' pupil, whilst those in urban and suburban working-class schools showed particular concern for the pupils' attainments and attitudes in the school.

In a study by Bacchus (1967) of the extent to which teachers in secondary modern schools tended to believe in the 'unfavourable' stereotype of these pupils, it was reported that teachers' attitudes were affected by the type of school they worked in and the area in which it was located. The most favourable attitudes to pupils came from male teachers in boys' schools, and those in 'middle-class' areas (as rated by the teacher). Probably the most interesting aspect of this study, however, is that Bacchus found consistent differences between teachers with favourable attitudes to pupils and those with unfavourable attitudes. The most significant determining factors were the personal attributes of the teacher. The more authoritarian teachers were more unfavourable in their assessment of the secondary modern pupil; teachers who were most critical of the pupils were in the youngest and oldest age groups.

This survey of previous research on teachers' attitudes to their work and to their pupils gives an indication of the importance of the social class of pupils and of the teachers' personalities as variables affecting ways in which pupils are assessed, and provides the background to the questions outlined in the Introduction to this study.

References

ALLEN, E. A. (1962). 'Professional training of teachers: a review of research', *Educ. Res.*, V, 3, 200-15.

ANDERSON, H. B. and BREWER, J. E. (1945-6). 'Studies in teachers' classroom personalities', *Applied Psy. Mono.*, no. 6, 8, 11.

BACCHUS, M. K. (1967). 'Some factors influencing the views of secondary modern school teachers on their pupils' interests and abilities', *Educ. Res.*, 9, 2, 147-50.

BLYTH, W. A. L. (1965). *English Primary Education*, Vols. I and II. London: Routledge.

BURT, C. (1937). *The Backward Child* (Revised 1961). London: University of London Press.

BUTCHER, H. J. (1965). 'The attitudes of student teachers to education: a comparison with the attitudes of experienced teachers and a study of changes during the training course', *Brit. J. Soc. Clin. Psychol.*, 4, 17-24.

COHEN, L. (1967). 'The teachers' role and liaison between school and neighbourhood'. In: CROFT, M., *et al.*, eds. *Linking Home and School*. London: Longmans.

DEPARTMENT OF EDUCATION AND SCIENCE: CENTRAL ADVISORY COUNCIL FOR EDUCATION (ENGLAND). (1967). *Children and their Primary Schools.* (Plowden Report). London: H.M. Stationery Office.

DOUGLAS, J. W. B. (1964). *The Home and the School.* London: MacGibbon & Kee.

EVANS, K. M. (1959a). 'Research on teaching ability', *Educ. Res.*, I, 3, 22-36.

EVANS, K. M. (1959b). 'The teacher-pupil relationship', *Educ. Res.*, II, 1, 3-8.

EVANS, K. M. (1966). 'The Minnesota Teacher Attitude Inventory', *Educ. Res.*, VIII, 2, 134-41.

EYSENCK, H. J. (1953). *The Structure of Human Personality.* London: Methuen; ch. 2.

FINLAYSON, D. S. and COHEN, L. (1967). 'The teacher's role: a comparative study of the conceptions of college of education students and head teachers', *Brit. J. Educ. Psychol.*, XXXVII, 1, 22-31.

FLOUD, J. (1962). 'Teaching in the affluent society', *Brit. J. Sociol.*, XIII, 4, 299-308.

FLOUD, J., HALSEY, A. H. and MARTIN, F. M. (1956). *Social Class and Educational Opportunity.* London: Heinemann.

FRASER, E. (1959). *Home Environment and the School.* London: University of London Press.

GLASS, R. (1948). *The Social Background of a Plan: A Study of Middlesbrough.* London: Routledge.

HALLWORTH, H. J. (1961). 'Teachers' personality ratings of high school pupils', *J. Educ. Psychol.*, 52, 297-302.

HALLWORTH, H. J. (1962). 'A teacher's perception of his pupil', *Educ. Rev.*, 14, 124-33.

HALLWORTH, H. J. (1965). 'Dimensions of personality and meaning', *Brit. J. Soc. Clin. Psychol.*, 4 (3), 161-8.

HALLWORTH, H. J. and MORRISON, A. (1964). 'A comparison of peer and teacher personality ratings of pupils in a secondary modern school', *Brit. J. Educ. Psychol.*, XXXIV, 3, 285-91.

HARDING, L. W. (1944a). 'A value-type generalizations test', *J. Soc. Psychol.*, 19, 53-79.

HARDING, L. W. (1944b). 'The value-type problemmaire', *J. Soc. Psychol.*, 19, 115-44.

HORN, J. L. and MORRISON, W. L. (1965). 'Dimensions of teacher attitudes', *J. Educ. Psychol.*, 56 (3), 118-25.

JONES, D. C. (1934). 'Social factors in secondary education'. In: *The Social Survey of Merseyside*, Vol. 3. London: Hodder & Stoughton; pp. 158-200.

JONES, J. (1966). 'Social class and the under-fives', *New Society*, 221, 935-6.

KERLINGER, F. N. and KAYA, E. (1959a). 'The construction and factor analytic validation of scales to measure attitudes toward education', *Educ. Psychol. Meas.*, 19, 13-29.

KERLINGER, F. N. and KAYA, E. (1959b). 'The predictive validity of scales constructed to measure attitudes toward education', *Educ. Psychol. Meas.*, 19, 305-17.

KOCH, H. L., *et al.* (1934). 'A scale for measuring attitude toward the question of children's freedom', *Child Develpm.*, 5, 253-66.

LEWIN, K., LIPPITT, R. and WHITE, R. (1939). 'Pattern of aggressive behaviour in experimentally created social climates', *J. of Soc. Psy.*, Vol. 10.

McINTYRE, D. and MORRISON, A. (1967). 'The educational opinions of teachers in training,' *Brit. J. Soc. Clin. Psychol.*, 6 (1), 32-7.

McINTYRE, D., MORRISON, A. and SUTHERLAND, J. (1966). 'Social and educational variables relating to teachers' assessments of primary school pupils', *Brit. J. Educ. Psychol.*, XXXVI, 3, 272-9.

MAYS, J. (1962). *Education and the Urban Child*. Liverpool: Liverpool University Press.

MINISTRY OF EDUCATION (1954). *Early Leaving*. A Report of the Central Advisory Council for Education (England). London: H.M. Stationery Office.

MORRISON, A., McINTYRE, D. and SUTHERLAND, J. (1965). 'Teachers' personality ratings of pupils in Scottish primary schools', *Brit. J. Educ. Psychol.*, XXXV, 3, 306-19.

MUSGROVE, F. (1961). 'Parents' expectations of the junior school', *Soc. Rev.*, Vol. 9, 167-80.

MUSGROVE, F. and TAYLOR, P. H. (1965). 'Teachers' and parents' conception of the teacher's role', *Brit. J. Educ. Psychol.*, XXXV, 2, 171-9.

OLIVER, R. A. C. and BUTCHER, H. J. (1962). 'Teachers' attitudes to education. The structure of educational attitudes', *Brit. J. Soc. Clin. Psychol.*, 1, 56-69.

RUDD, W. G. A. and WISEMAN, S. (1962). 'Sources of dissatisfaction among a group of teachers', *Brit. J. Educ. Psychol.*, XXXII, 3, 275-91.

SWIFT, D. F. (1967). 'Family environment and 11+ success: some basic predictors', *Brit. J. Educ. Psychol.*, XXXVII (1), 10-21.

TAYLOR, P. H. (1962). 'Children's evaluations of the characteristics of a good teacher', *Brit. J. Educ. Psychol.*, XXXII, 3, 258-66.

TUPPIN, C. J. S. (1966). 'The measurement of teachers' attitudes', *Educ. Res.*, VIII, 2, 142-5.

WEBB, J. (1962). 'The sociology of a school', *Brit. J. Sociol.*, XIII, 3, 264-72.

WILSON, B. R. (1962). 'The teachers' role—a sociological analysis', *Brit. J. Sociol.*, XIII, 1, 15-32.

WISEMAN, S. (1964). *Education and Environment*. Manchester: Manchester University Press.

CHAPTER II

Sources of Information

A S has already been explained in the Introduction, this study of teachers' attitudes is the second part of the three-stage project 'Teaching Beginners to Read'. The means of selecting the schools and the representativeness of the groups of schools at each stage are described in detail in the first report of the research findings,[1] and a summary of the information on selection of schools is included in the description of the stages of the reading inquiry given in this report in Appendix A, pp. 77-8. Briefly, the schools in the research were representative of London primary schools generally in relation to school organization, religious denomination, and social area.

The information used in the teachers' attitudes study came from three sources:

1. *The teachers*

    (a) Information regarding the teachers' opinions, attitudes and estimates of pupils *generally* and *individually* in relation to aspects of pupils' home conditions, attributes and other characteristics, was obtained by means of four written questionnaires: an *Initial Questionnaire;* a *Home Background* (*General*) form; a *Home Background* (*Individual*) form; and a *Teacher's Personal Questionnaire.*

    (b) The teachers' estimates and predictions of *individual* pupils reading readiness, attainment and progress were obtained by the use of two rating forms: *Reading Readiness estimate; Primer Criterion.*

    (c) Information concerning their age, teaching experience, social class origin, etc. was supplied by teachers who completed a *Personal Questionnaire.*

2. *The pupils*

    Their reading attainment according to a NFER survey test, described in Appendix C, page 121.

[1] GOODACRE, E. J. (1967). *Reading in Infant Classes.* Slough: NFER.

3. *The school and its environment*

Information regarding the type of school organization (whether infant only, or junior mixed and infant), and the school's social area. (Census data regarding distribution of occupations by social class categories for the school's catchment area, *not* an estimate by the head of pupils' parental occupations.)

Table C/I in Appendix C (p. 122), shows the parts of the inquiry which were used in this second report on attitudes; the numbers of schools and teachers completing each part; the numbers of children for whom estimates and test scores were available at each stage of the research.

Questionnaires and rating forms

Six types of forms were completed by the teachers. Four were concerned primarily with the teachers' attitudes towards and opinions about pupils' home background; and two with their observations and predictions regarding pupils' reading readiness, attainment and progress.

Copies of these six forms appear in Appendix B (pp. 79-120) together with a brief description of the design of each form, the area of information it covered, the numbers and types of teachers completing it and certain other relevant details.

Several points should be stressed about the information used in this attitude study:

(a) The questionnaires and forms used provided *written* information about the teachers' opinions and ratings of their pupils. Thus we know only what these teachers thought about certain subjects and how they viewed particular pupils. This information cannot tell us whether the pupils actually possessed certain attributes, personality characteristics, etc. With one exception, the teachers are the sole source of information for the pupils, and as the outline of previous research has shown, this type of data may be subject to distortion because of the operation of various factors, such as the teacher's beliefs about the social class composition of the school, the teacher's age and experience, or the sex of the pupils and the teacher's attitude to this factor. The only objective measure of pupils' attainment used was that of their scores on a reading attainment test. Where a distinction has been made between pupils' *estimated* and *tested* attainment, the former refers to the teachers' assessment of their pupils' attainments in reading based on the

10

book each pupil had reached in the reading scheme used in the school. *Tested* attainment was the pupil's score on the reading test.

(b) The written information obtained from the teachers took several forms. Sometimes they were asked for factual information about themselves, and to answer they had only to select the appropriate category on the questionnaire. Other questions were open-ended, and the teachers' answers could be brief or expansive according to their feelings about the subject. In these latter cases, the teachers' answers had to be analysed and coded into appropriate groupings by the research worker. Sometimes the teachers were given a list of items and asked to rate them in order of importance, so indicating the intensity of their feelings about particular aspects. In relation to their assessments of pupils, they were asked either to judge the pupils as a group, or to rate them in relation to one another within the class group, or answer (for each pupil) whether they had or had not observed particular listed types of behaviour or attributes.

Procedure

The teachers' answers were examined generally, and then analysed in relation to four factors to see whether there were variations in relation to either the type of school, or the type of teacher.

Environmental variables

The two environmental factors were (1) the type of social class composition of the school's catchment area, referred to as the school's *social area*, and (2) the type of *school organization* (infants only school, i.e. no children over age seven, or junior and infants combined, i.e. children in the same school till age eleven).

(1) *Social area.* The objective measure of the social area was based on data from the 1951 Census figures. The method of calculation and detailed description of the social areas are described in Appendix C, (pp. 121-4). Schools were grouped into three broad social groupings, characterized as follows:

Social Area I Lower working-class; mainly partly skilled and unskilled occupations; densely residential and industrial.

11

> *Social Area II* Working-class; skilled and partly skilled occupa-
> tions; some socially ambitious families keen to
> move out of a densely residential area.
>
> *Social Area III* Suburban/middle-class; more 'white collar' occu-
> pations; less densely populated.

School *social area* was considered in order to see to what extent and
in what particular ways the social class composition of the locality
affected the teachers' opinions and ratings.

(2) *Organization* was the other school variable considered, because
the infant only schools tended to be larger with more pupils on the
roll, and it was argued that as a consequence the teachers in the
smaller junior mixed and infant schools might have closer contacts
with pupils' homes with access to more intimate knowledge of pupils
and their parents than would be the case in the larger organization.
(It should be noted that there was no significant difference between
the two types of school in regard to teacher/pupil ratio.)

Teacher variables

Two teacher variables were considered; (1) the teachers' *position*
in the school (head or class teacher) and (2) their own social background or *social class origin*.

(1) *The teacher's position* was thought to be important because of
differences in relation to role and function in the school. For
instance, Heads would probably have frequent but rather formal
contacts with parents, whereas class teachers would have more
indirect opportunities, such as the 'News' period, for gaining impressions of pupils' home background.

(2) *The teacher's social class origin* was studied because, although
one would expect that teachers would predominantly have middle-
class values [as has been suggested by Jackson and Marsden (1962)]
by reason of their professional standing, there might be particular
questions or aspects of the subject where differences in background
and upbringing were apparent. Information about the teachers'
social class origin was only available for those teachers who completed a *Personal Questionnaire*. Two groupings were used: middle-
class and working-class. Details of the classification used, the
distribution of the women class teachers' social class origins, and a
comparison of these figures with those from a national survey are
included in Appendix C (pp. 124-6).

It should be noted that it was not always possible to examine particular information in respect to all four variables, as in some instances the numbers were too small or the variable did not apply; for example, only class teachers completed estimates for individual children, so analysis in relation to the teachers' position was not applicable.

Table C/IV, Appendix C (p. 126) shows the distribution of schools by organization and social area, and the position and social class origin of the teachers completing each part of the attitude study.

References

GOODACRE, E. J. (1967). *Reading in Infant Classes.* Slough: NFER.
JACKSON, B. and MARSDEN, D. (1962). *Education and the Working Class.* London: Routledge.

NOTE: STATISTICAL AND EDUCATIONAL SIGNIFICANCE

The statistical convention has been adopted that all differences reported between groups in relation to the variables studied, are those which are significant at or above the 5% level of significance; where the level reached 1% or 0·1% it has been described as 'very significant'. This means that the results reported are unlikely to have arisen by chance, and the differences would therefore appear to be real. The use of the words 'significant' or 'very significant' indicates the degree of confidence one may have in the reality of the difference, depending on whether the result could have arisen by chance one in twenty times (5% level), or only once in a hundred (1% level) or once in a thousand (0·1% level).

Logically, we have first to establish the reality of the difference, the possibility of such a result occurring by chance, and then to estimate its *educational* importance or significance. We need some evidence as to the reality of the difference, but its *importance* must be decided in the light of our experience and knowledge of the particular circumstances. It is quite possible for a difference which may be highly significant in educational terms to be indicated by a quite small statistical difference. Conversely, a highly significant statistical difference may draw attention to a spurious association, leading straight to an educational 'blind alley'.

Finally, it should be noted that where the symbol % has been used this signifies the level of statistical significance, whilst the words 'per cent' have been used when reference is being made to the number of teachers or pupils in every hundred answering in a particular way, showing a certain characteristic, etc.

CHAPTER III

The Main Findings

THIS chapter summarizes the main findings of the second stage of the inquiry, in terms of the questions listed on page xiii of the Introduction. The findings are discussed more fully in the following chapters, and statistical evidence and analysis are given in the Appendices.

1. *What importance do infant teachers attach to pupils' home background in the teaching of reading?*

Generally the teachers considered that the pupils' home background was an important factor in learning to read; they described those aspects of the home which they believed could actively assist that process, and the abilities pupils used in learning to read which they most readily associated with differences in home conditions. They most valued the provision of suitable reading material in pupils' homes on which pupils could practise their newly acquired skill, and the type of atmosphere in which it was taken for granted by parents and child that reading was a desirable skill to be acquired. Differences in home background were most readily connected with a child's desire to learn to read and his rate of learning.

2. *How do teachers categorize their pupils in relation to home background.*

The teachers in this study appeared to be familiar with the terms 'good' and 'poor' homes as a means of categorizing pupils. When asked to describe them in their own words, they used more motivational and cultural characteristics in describing the 'good' home. The 'good' home tended to be described as one which facilitated the teacher's task of instruction by preparing the child for participation in the formal learning situation and also for acceptance of the teacher's role in it. If a child showed no eagerness to learn to read, teachers believed that the difficulty of imparting the techniques of the skill was increased, because not only did they have to provide the appropriate systematic instruction (difficult enough if teacher and pupil used different types of language systems, dialect, etc.) but they had also to demonstrate to pupils that reading was a desirable and necessary skill.

15

When teachers rated the different characteristics of a 'good' home, the school's social area assumed importance. For instance, there was little difference between the ratings of teachers in middle and upper working-class areas, but particular motivational and cultural items assumed importance as distinguishing characteristics between the two working-class groups. These items were the ability of the parents to answer their children's questions, to provide stimulating experiences in the home and to help with school work; parents' own levels of education and intelligence, and the presence of 'good' conversation and manners in the home. Comparing the extreme social area groups, the items regarded as most important were a religious faith, parental help with school work, stable emotional home life, and a mother who did not go out to work.

Each teacher's ratings for the various items were added up to give a total score for this question, and if high scores can be interpreted as indicative of an interest in the contribution of the 'good' home, it seems likely that such an interest is related to the individual teacher's age and general personality type. The findings suggest that it is more likely to be the older or more authoritarian type of teacher, with unfavourable attitudes to pupils and their homes, who is most likely to categorize pupils in terms of 'good' or 'poor' homes.

3. *What is the extent of teachers' personal contacts with pupils and their homes, and what clues do they use as a basis for their impressions of pupils' home conditions?*

It was found that amongst these urban infant teachers, contacts with parents seldom extended beyond meetings on school premises. Few school heads had established parent-teacher organizations, and few teachers ever visited pupils' homes. Two out of three parents[1] were said to visit the school, usually for reasons connected with the child's physical well-being, and since these questions were asked of teachers of young children, parental interest at this stage was largely an expression of maternal concern.

---

[1] Since one in three parents are not seen by the teachers at school (even from the beginning of the child's schooling), one wonders to what extent lack of face-to-face relationships influences the teachers' assessments of parental interest —it may well be that the unknown, unmet parent soon comes to be regarded as the parent who 'takes little interest'. Douglas (1964) assessed parental encouragement by using the class teachers' comments at the end of the first and fourth years in the primary school and their records of the number of times parents visited the school to discuss their children's progress. It was found that on the basis of this assessment of parental interest, when parents took little interest, their children lost ground in tests and gained rather fewer places in the selection examinations than would have been expected from their measured ability.

Pupils' records of attendance and lateness were not indicative of social class differences in attitudes towards the value of education, but pupils' reasons for being away or their excuses for lateness provided teachers, to some extent, with information about the pupils' home circumstances. There was, however, some evidence to suggest that certain types of schools might find particular reasons more 'acceptable' than others.

Teachers seemed to have little difficulty in finding evidence of a child's economic circumstances. Conversations, class 'News', or actual observations of personal belongings, etc. brought to school were considered to be indications of a family's pattern of conspicuous consumption. The type and quality of a child's clothing, even in today's welfare state, still seems to be a major 'clue' for most teachers. Obvious signs such as the bare feet of the nineteen-thirties have disappeared, but indications such as the suitability of clothing from the point of view of climate and weather conditions, and the care and quality of underclothing provide a basis for comparison to the practised eye of the observer.

The teachers suggested a variety of ways in which the actions of parents could be construed as constituting parental interest in the child's reading progress. However, analysis of their answers indicated areas of difference which could well be the basis of misunderstandings between teachers and parents. There were, for instance, the different responses to the practical suggestion that parents should provide pupils with a copy of the reader in the school reading scheme, so that the child could practise at home. Firstly, provision of the reader and parents 'hearing' their children read at home was more often suggested as a sign of parental interest by the heads than by the class teachers. Secondly, the head's views as to whether the parent was expected to borrow or to buy the book appeared to be related to his own social class origin. A head of working-class origin would be likely to consider a request from a parent to borrow a school reader as a sign of interest, but the same request to a head of middle-class origin might be considered as a 'trivial' reason for a visit to the school.[1]

---

[1] DEPARTMENT OF EDUCATION AND SCIENCE (1967). 'National Survey of Parental Attitudes and Circumstances Related to School and Pupil Characteristics', Appendix 3, *Children and their Primary Schools* (Plowden Report) reported that just over a third of the parents had *bought* copies, to have at home, of some of the textbooks their children were using at school. Considerably higher proportions of parents from the non-manual than manual worker families had bought textbooks.

B

There was evidence to suggest that the type of school organization has a bearing on the role expected of parents. For instance, more heads of the smaller, combined department school expected parents to take an active interest in the work of the school to the extent of visiting the school to ask about the methods in use, whereas more class teachers in the infant only schools emphasized the parents' supportive role, expecting them to encourage and sustain their children in their efforts but not, at this early stage in their children's education, to want to help with school work.

4. *If paternal occupation is used as a criterion for assessing pupils' home background, how reliable are teachers as 'judges'?*

The findings were that teachers' estimates were least reliable in the lowest social areas, probably because they were unfamiliar with the degrees of responsibility or training involved in manual occupations, and were less likely to be informed about the educational requirements or intellectual concomitants and responsibilities of the newer professions and the more recently developed occupations in technology. Also, these teachers appeared to have certain predetermined notions about the type of occupations associated with particular regions, and these assumptions had considerable influence —even to the extent of being sometimes more effective than the actual recorded occupations of pupils' fathers. The evidence was not conclusive, but it seemed likely that where records of paternal occupations were not kept, teachers' inferences about the incidence of particular occupations in certain regions were less in evidence. However, in these circumstances the head's own social class background appeared to assume more importance—he tended to see the social composition of his school more in terms of his own social class origin.

5. *What inferences do teachers make about pupils whose parents follow different types of occupation?*

The teachers' lack of knowledge regarding the gradients of status in the manual classes was reflected in the tendency for teachers in lower working-class areas to see their classes as homogeneous groups, and pupils as predominantly children of fathers with manual occupations. Their tendency to stress the power and responsibility of occupations which, in the past, were related to educational mobility and hence intellectual capacity, also led them to think of pupils from the lower working-class areas not only as *socially* homogeneous groups, but also as being *intellectually* homogeneous; more teachers in the lower working-class areas tended to accept that they had no pupils of above average intellectual ability. Further, it appeared from the teachers' comments that their own language system and academically biased education might make it extremely difficult for many of them to recognize unfamiliar forms of intellectual functioning.

6. *To what extent do such inferences affect teachers' ratings of individual pupils?*

In reply to the request to complete estimates, records and predictions of individual pupils' abilities, attributes, reading attainment and progress, it was found that the teachers in the extreme social areas were less reluctant to supply information about pupils' home conditions than the teachers in the upper working-class areas. This suggested that the teachers in the extreme social areas tended to have well-structured stereotypes of the type of pupil and home they could expect. It seemed likely that these expectations were related to their ideas concerning the relationship of occupational level, social conditions and intellectual ability.

Nevertheless, when the teachers were asked to rate pupils' personal attributes, school organization rather than social area appeared to be the effective factor. The teachers in the infant only schools tended to describe pupils in more positive terms and generally seemed to favour slightly different personality characteristics from those favoured by teachers in the combined department schools.

Again, it was noticeable that the teachers in the upper working-class areas had greater difficulty in completing the assessments of environmental conditions affecting progress in reading. Teachers in infant only schools also seemed more reluctant to assess pupils in relation to the quality of their homes and the amount of parental interest, possibly because the teachers in these schools generally seemed to expect less overt signs of parental interest than did those working in the smaller combined department schools. The infant only teachers, therefore, had less concrete evidence on which to base their judgements.

The fact that more lower working-class area pupils were rated as being fond of school and, in regard to intellectual ability, were not estimated significantly differently from pupils in other areas (although on the basis of the teacher's general estimates of pupils' intellectual ability, these pupils had shown as markedly inferior), suggested that the teachers of these pupils may have lowered their standards of assessment; that is, normalized a lower level of ability in relation to their inferences about pupils from these social areas.

Evidence from the teachers' reading-readiness estimates of pupils, suggested that the teachers in the upper working-class areas, in comparison with those in the lower working-class areas, tended to provide more opportunities for assessing pupils' perceptual development and were less likely to wait for pupils' 'readiness'. Their pupils' initial enthusiasm appeared to be steadily maintained and by their second year of schooling, they were well established in the basic pre-reading skills and receiving systematic reading instruction (letter sounds and names) and so were able to attempt unknown words for themselves and to proceed at their own pace. By the second year the lower working-class pupils were undoubtedly showing enthusiasm for acquiring the skill, and possibly within a year the difference between the two groups would have been less marked. However, by the second year the approach of transfer to the junior stage of schooling appeared to affect the judgements of the teachers of the lower group, so that they were beginning to use more uniform criteria, e.g. estimates of pupils' progress and chances of success. We do not know to what extent teachers in junior schools in different areas make inferences about the different social classes and adopt diverging standards, but it seems clear that the teachers of the top infant classes react as if they believe that junior teachers will not diverge in their standards, but will rather apply uniform 'junior school standards'.[1]

7. *Do teachers of infants have certain distinctive social and psychological characteristics, distinguishing them from teachers of older children in the educational system, which would be of importance in considering teachers' attitudes to pupils and their homes?*

This study provided further evidence of the previously reported high level of professional satisfaction shown by infant teachers. Previous research indicated that, as a group, infant teachers had

[1] The continuing influence of the 1931 Report of the Consultative Committee on the Primary School, reprinted as recently as 1962, may have encouraged the use of uniform criteria of assessment by teachers in the junior school, since it gave the impression that the main task of the junior school teacher was to develop pupils' reading comprehension. It suggested that few children, except for a few backward ones, would require systematic instruction after the age of seven, and therefore the implication was that top infants would achieve a specific standard irrespective of length of infant schooling or social background.

outstandingly good personal relationships *in school*. The present study suggested that the class teachers found their greatest satisfaction in their relationships with the children rather than with adults (colleagues or parents), whilst the major dissatisfactions were the low status accorded to infant teachers by the community[1] and the lack of opportunities for intellectual development.

These infant teachers saw themselves as cheerful, conscientious, sensible and adaptable. They believed their principle deficiencies were lack of ambition, originality, confidence and foresight. Their social background was mainly that of the intermediate and skilled occupational levels, and they tended to be predominantly 'first generation' professionals. It was not surprising, therefore, to find that they did not read widely in a vocational sense; but perhaps the most important implication of their social background lies in the fact that as a group within the education system they are likely to be verbally less fluent and articulate, less capable of putting ideas into words and arguing convincingly, which may be important considerations when they need to act as spokesmen for their pupils' educational needs. There was evidence to suggest that it was the Heads who were more likely to be aware that such social and psychological characteristics acted as limitations on the scope of their role.

8. *How far are differences in teachers' attitudes to pupils' home background related to psychological rather than sociological factors?*

Whilst the infant teachers appeared generally to attach considerable importance to environmental factors, the way in which they reacted to these professional or group generalizations and the extent to which they used them—imposing preconceived and stereotyped categories upon their experiences with pupils and parents—were more likely to be related to their own basic personality. It was the more authoritarian type of teacher who tended to have an unfavourable

---

[1] Bacchus (1967) reported that the male teachers in secondary modern schools with unfavourable views of their pupils tended to be 'more dissatisfied with what they got out of the job in terms of status, salary, opportunities for promotion, etc.'. It should be noted that in the present study with *infant* teachers, the association between teachers' attitudes to pupils and homes and their satisfaction with their status in the community, did not reach a statistically significant relationship. Generally, these infant teachers seemed to be relatively uninterested in opportunities for promotion. Only in regard to the *heads* was it found that those dissatisfied with their status appeared to be less optimistic about the school's power to change pupils' values (5 % level of significance).

attitude towards pupils' home backgrounds,[1] particularly in relation to pupils' parents. They were also more likely to feel pessimistic about the school's ability to change pupils' values.

Generally, heads had more favourable attitudes to pupils than had the class teachers, and the attitudes of women heads were more favourable than those of men heads. Teachers who preferred teaching pupils individually rather than in groups, tended to be more favourably disposed towards their pupils and their types of background.

9. *Do the personality and attitudes of the head have any direct bearing on the level of pupils' reading attainment?*

A head's personality did not appear to be related to his school's standards or to the staff records of pupils' progress or reading achievement; but there may perhaps be an indirect relationship, through the medium of the head's attitudes to pupils and their homes, which could affect the staff's morale and consequently their expectations of pupils' future achievements. It seemed likely that a head's attitudes to pupils and their home backgrounds assumed most importance in relation to schools in the lower working-class areas. The head's personality and attitudes may well be a crucial factor in determining the extent to which his staff are able to 'break through the barrier of IQ depression'[2] which tends to operate so strongly in these areas.

10. *To what extent are these findings affected by (a) the type of organization of the school in which the teacher works; (b) the teacher's position in the school; (c) the teacher's own social class origin?*

(a) Some of the differences reported in relation to school organization were undoubtedly related to the distinguishing organizational

---

[1] These findings, that infant teachers' attitudes to pupils' home background are significantly associated with the personality dimension of authoritarianism, agree with those of Bacchus (1967) in relation to male teachers in the secondary modern school.

[2] Professor Kenneth B. Clark used this phrase in *Education in Depressed Areas* (1963) when describing the crucial role of the school in determining the level of scholastic achievement. He argues that standards and quality of education need not be lowered by the limitations set by home conditions; far more significant were the *general attitudes of teachers toward their pupils and the manner in which these were communicated.* Too many teachers, Clark suggested, maintain 'the pervasive and archaic belief that children from culturally deprived backgrounds are by virtue of their deprivation or *lower status position* inherently ineducable'. He proposes that schools 'break through the barrier of IQ depression', since many ideas about the absolute nature of intelligence are more relevant to assumptions about class than about education.

characteristics of school size and pupil range. The infant only schools tend to have more pupils on roll, and their teachers have only a short period in which to become acquainted with pupils, so it is not surprising to find that the teachers in these schools experienced more difficulties in completing assessments about pupils' home conditions. However, there may be a further reason. The infant school philosophy of education may be more pervasive in the single department school, and since one of its basic tenets is the importance of the needs of the individual child, this may mean that less emphasis is being placed upon group relationships—pupils, parents, teachers. Certainly there was evidence that the teachers in the infant only schools were less concerned about overt signs of parental interest, of parents being interested in the *school's* methods and activities. They may, of course, be more prepared to approach parents and to provide them with information. They seemed to take up a more positive approach towards both pupils and parents. They were probably less interested in achieving parental approval of their approach and methods than in ensuring that parents appreciated and encouraged their children's efforts, thus strengthening pupils' motivation to learn.

The findings of the present study suggest that the combined department school may more nearly resemble the traditional school system developed in the past in which the role of socialization tends to be of primary importance, whereas the infant only schools seem to develop an autonomous role, thereby cutting across local traditional reactions and possibly facilitating social change. How much these basic differences can be related to the organizational factors of school size and age range of pupils and how much to the generally ignored fact that infant only schools are staffed solely by women under a woman head, would seem to require further research. It can be stated, however, that there were no significant differences between the attitudes of the teachers working in the two types of schools. Again, further research would be necessary to evaluate the importance of the finding in relation to heads, which indicated that they had more favourable attitudes towards pupils, and that women heads had more favourable attitudes than men.

(b) Where differences existed in relation to the teacher's position, they appeared to be mainly the result of differences in the degree of contact with parents and pupils respectively. For instance, more heads described the 'good' home in emotional and moral terms, since they were often more aware than the class teacher of the parents' personal problems and were therefore in a better position to realize the importance of an emotionally stable home for both personality development and scholastic progress of pupils. More heads mentioned parents' attendance at Open days as a sign of parental interest, since, for them, this offered clear evidence of an additional visit made out of interest and not simply because of admission requirements. Too much weight should not be given to this point, but the reception class teachers' answers gave the impression that many of them felt that parents only came to school to see *them* about lost property!

As has been previously noted, the existence of footwear and a pupil's general physical appearance were formerly considered to be the most reliable 'clues' to the economic circumstances of the home, whereas today the quality and condition of pupils' clothing, particularly underclothing, may assume more importance. The latter is more likely to be seen by the class teacher when supervising pupils' changing for physical training. Heads, however, appear to be more likely to rely upon their observations of parents for their 'clues'. In these circumstances the attitudes of the heads towards parents may have a more profound effect than those of their staff. One thinks, for instance, of the head who makes rules and tries rigidly to control the conditions of parents' visiting the school—an action which, in itself, may be a factor which contributes to the formation of parental and neighbourhood opinion. Since parental esteem is the head's main 'feedback' for awareness of his authority and prestige in the area, it is his actions in relation to parents in particular which will directly affect his status and satisfaction with his role. That this can be a vicious circle is probably exemplified by the case of the authoritarian head whose characteristic attitudes tend to antagonize parents, thereby bringing about the very social isolation which this type of personality fears.

(c) In comparison with the other three variables, the factor of social class origin appeared to have much less effect. It seemed that generally these teachers had adopted the middle-class values associated with their profession. When differences occurred, they related to attitudes concerning the use of money. Although teachers with a working-class background appeared to have adopted the cultural values of the social class to which they aspired, they retained their original attitudes towards money. Probably their upbringing was characterized by financial difficulties, and entry to a higher social class involved for most a fight against economic odds.[1]

Differences in attitude towards the use of money may explain some differences in practice between teachers. One example brought to light in this study concerns the provision of the school reader for practice at home; teachers of working-class origin probably assume that parents would borrow a copy if they wanted one, whereas the middle-class teacher would expect the copy to be bought. There are probably other instances of differences and misunderstandings between school and home, which in fact involve differences in 'values' in the monetary sense rather than in the sense of moral principles.

References

BACCHUS, M. K. (1967). 'Some factors influencing the views of secondary modern school teachers on their pupils' interests and abilities', *Educ. Res.*, 9, 2, 147-50.

CLARK, K. B. (1963). 'Educational stimulation of racially disadvantaged children'. In: PASSOW, A. H. ed. *Education in Depressed Areas.* New York: Bureau of Publications, Teachers College, Columbia University.

DEPARTMENT OF EDUCATION AND SCIENCE: CENTRAL ADVISORY COUNCIL FOR EDUCATION (ENGLAND). (1967). 'The 1964 National Survey: survey among parents of primary school children by Roma Morton-William, The Government Social Survey', Appendix 3. In: *Children and their Primary Schools.* London: H.M. Stationery Office.

DOUGLAS, J. W. B. (1964). *The Home and the School.* London: MacGibbon & Kee.

KLEIN, J. (1967). 'The parents of school children'. In: CROFT, M. *et al.* eds. *Linking Home and School.* London: Longmans.

[1] Josephine Klein (1967) has outlined some of the differences which distinguish the traditional 'roughs' in the working class from the 'respectable' working-class family. Presumably most teachers with a working-class origin would tend to come from the latter type of home. In this connection, Klein makes an interesting point when she describes how the 'respectable' family takes pains to achieve standards of domestic behaviour and social interaction which will distinguish them from the 'roughs' amongst whom they live. However, the children in these families are brought up with the knowledge that the 'roughs' are 'different' from them in only style of life—but not in economic circumstances—and that a period of illness or unemployment or some other misfortune may be sufficient to push a whole family below the poverty line.

B*

CHAPTER IV

Pupils' Home Background

I do not really feel that a teacher gets an absolutely true picture of her children's background. Some parents she never meets at all and most information is derived from the children; the child usually remembers only the most vivid details to report, forgetting their routine activities.

(Class teacher, lower working-class area school).

A. 'Good' and 'Poor' Homes

Procedure

IN the *Initial Questionnaire*, heads and class teachers were asked to give their opinions regarding the part a child's home background plays in the initial stages of learning to read, and to describe the characteristics of a 'good' and 'poor' home respectively. These three open-ended questions provided useful information about the importance teachers attach to different aspects of pupils' home background.

The next stage was to obtain information regarding the order of importance teachers assigned to these items, and to discover whether particular items assumed more importance in certain circumstances. A checklist of 34 items was devised, using those items suggested by the teachers in their answers to the open-ended questions. This checklist was included in the *Home Background (General)* form completed by the infant staff of schools taking part in the second year of the follow-up study. All heads and infant teachers were asked to rate each item on a five-point scale (high values indicating importance) in the light of their experience with present pupils.

Finally, the teachers' total scores on this rating question were examined in relation to the school and teacher variables, and also included as a variable in both item analyses used in connection with the teachers' attitudes scales.

Pupils' Home Background

Findings: 1. Open-ended Questions

Home background and learning to read. The teachers' answers to the first question—about the part a child's home background plays in learning to read—provided information on three aspects of the problem: (a) the importance of the factor of home background in teaching beginners; (b) the aspects of the *home* which help a child learn to read; and (c) the abilities or attributes required by pupils in learning to read which are related to home conditions.

(a) Half the teachers emphasized the importance of pupils' homes in teaching reading, and only five teachers (four heads and one class teacher) commented that they believed it to be unimportant, stressing instead the importance of regular attendance and continuity of schooling. One wrote: 'The best readers do not always come from the best homes', and another said that the teacher 'may have to save the child from boredom induced by an over-keen parent'.

(b) The aspects of the *home* singled out for comment were, in order of frequency mentioned:
1. reading material
2. parental interest in reading
3. home's encouragement and co-operation with the school
4. parental conversation
5. practice of reading to children
6. the richness of home experience
7. the emotional security of the home
8. early pre-reading experiences such as parents discussing pictures and stories
9. the discipline and routine in the home.

(c) The pupils' abilities or attributes mentioned in order of frequency were:
1. their attitude to learning to read
2. their rate of learning
3. their reading readiness
4. their attitude to school and learning generally
5. their emotional stability
6. their general knowledge
7. their grasp of the relationship between the spoken and written word.

Abilities and attributes which help to facilitate progress in the initial stages of learning to read are varied, but can be grouped, broadly speaking, into three distinct categories: intellectual, physical and personal qualities. Inglis (1948) considers that the intellectual qualities include 'intelligence, vocabulary, ability to judge'. The physical qualities refer to 'health and the sensory and perceptual development of vision, hearing and motor control; personal qualities consist of emotional stability, social adjustment and desirable attitudes towards the achievement of reading skill'. It is interesting that in the present study, when teachers referred to pupils' personal qualities, more than half thought of attitude towards acquiring the skill as being related to home factors, whilst few teachers mentioned emotional stability and none referred to physical qualities.

School and teacher differences. There were not many differences—fewer heads of junior mixed and infant schools mentioned 'home encouragement' and 'child's attitude to school'; noticeably more class teachers working in middle-class area schools referred to appropriate reading material.

Fewer class teachers mentioned parental interest in books or pupils' 'reading readiness' but not as many heads referred to the parental practice of reading to children or the level of parental conversation. It is possible that class teachers considered that pupils' willingness to learn the skill implied 'reading readiness', whereas the heads, whilst frequently using the term, seldom described the characteristics which they associated with it.

Teachers' concepts of 'good' and 'poor' homes

It was possible to group the attributes the teachers used to describe a 'good' home into the following eight categories: motivational; emotional; cultural; material; moral; organizational (including regularity); economic; and parental interest in school progress.[1]

[1] 'Cultural' was used for those items where the teacher's use implied that standards were associated with a higher social grouping or that there was an absolute standard by which behaviour could be judged; 'regularity', those items which emphasized regularity in child-rearing practices, etc.; 'economic' for conditions such as housing and employment, etc.; 'parental interest in school progress' was used for items describing school and home co-operation, as well as interest in child's general activities as distinct from interest in child's *general* activities classified under 'motivational'.

Approximately half the items mentioned by the teachers could be classified under the headings of motivational and emotional. Tables D/I and D/II in Appendix D, (pp. 128-9) show the teachers' views on the characteristics of 'good' and 'poor' homes respectively, classified into these different categories. When the items mentioned in the definitions of 'good' and 'poor' homes were compared, significantly more items of a motivational and cultural nature were mentioned in relation to a 'good' home whilst more moral material and economic items were used by the teachers to describe the 'poor' home.

These findings suggest that teachers tend to think of the 'good' home as the one which facilitates their task[1]—the home in which parents are able to assist in the mental development of their children. The implication is that the parents in such homes possess the *ability* to help their children. The teachers' answers gave the impression that they were assuming parents had the educational experience, the physical energy and the time to take an active and determining role in the development of their children's cognitive powers, particularly through the medium of language. Many of these teachers showed approval of the home which encouraged children to use an elaborated rather than a restricted linguistic code of the type described by Bernstein (1961, 1962).[2] Since, as Bernstein has suggested, working-class children are more likely to use the latter, and since parents in certain occupations are likely to be better educated and to have more opportunities of helping their children, teachers of young children may be equating the 'good' home with middle-class values, and

---

[1] Musgrove and Taylor (1965) reported that the teachers in their study saw their work primarily in intellectual and moral terms.

[2] Typical examples were as follows:

'Time given to children by parents, e.g. talking, explaining things, telling stories' —class teacher in a lower working-class school.

'Homes where children learn to express themselves well'—head of working-class origin, in a working-class school.

'Quiet periods of relaxation, when parents talk with their families about current events and each others' problems'—Head of working-class origin in lower working-class school.

'Where the child is talked to, listened to and conversed with and where emphasis is placed correctly on the value of the written word'—Head of working-class origin in lower working-class school.

'A home where there is an encouraging and sympathetic attitude towards the awakening mind rather than only a concern with material comforts'—class teacher in working-class school.

'Where parents are interested in the progress of the children and capable of helping them'—class teacher in lower working-class school.

therefore be discriminating against working-class children and their parents as Jackson and Marsden (1962) suggested could be the case amongst teachers in the grammar schools.

The teachers' answers suggested that their use of the term 'poor' had two slightly different connotations; they could mean either having little money, or deserving of pity and unfortunate.

School and teacher differences. At this stage, school organization was not included in the analysis, but in relation to the other three variables, the only differences were that significantly more heads mentioned material and organizational aspects in describing the 'good' home and emphasized emotional and moral aspects in referring to 'poor' homes. In describing the 'good' home, teachers in lower working-class schools emphasized organization and featured material aspects more prominently than did teachers in middle-class area schools.

Findings: 2. Rating Question

When the teachers were asked to rate the different items which had been suggested as characteristic of a 'good' home, the rank order of the categories based on the teachers' responses 'important' or 'very important' showed a correlation of ·71 with the rank order established from the earlier classification based on the open-ended question. (See Table D/III in Appendix D, p. 130).

Table IV/A shows the mean rating of the items in the check-list by all the teachers.

School and teacher differences. When comparisons were made between the answers of teachers working in schools in lower working- and middle-class areas, it was noticeable that particular characteristics assumed more importance in certain areas. There was relatively little difference between the ratings of the middle- and working-class area teachers—the latter attached more importance to parents' ability to answer their children's questions, whereas middle-class area teachers rated the item 'a religious faith' more highly. Comparing the two working-class areas, teachers in the higher social area attached more importance to the motivational and cultural items—'parents answer children's questions', 'stimulate and help children carry out their ideas', 'good conversation' and, particularly, parents' 'intelligence and education', 'help with school work' and 'good manners'.

TABLE IV/A: *Mean Rating by All Teachers (N=275) of Items Describing the 'Good' Home*

ITEM SUGGESTED BY TEACHERS AS CHARACTERISTIC OF THE 'GOOD' HOME	MEAN
Child loved and wanted for own sake (B[1])	4·91
Mother working but makes provision (G)	4·83
Home life stable (B)	4·81
Children have adequate sleep (H)	4·73
Firm but kindly discipline (E)	4·71
Sense of moral and spiritual values (E)	4·71
Family united and mutually considerate (B)	4·68
Parents interested in child's activities (C)	4·67
Parents talk and read to child (C)	4·67
Children adequately clothed, fed (H)	4·53
Parents show an interest in child's school progress (A)	4·47
Parents answer questions (C)	4·46
Meals, sleep, habits regular (D)	4·43
Familiarity with books, reading, etc. (F)	4·38
Good, sensible food (H)..	4·30
Good manners and social habits (F)	4·26
Cleanliness (D)	4·23
Television watching supervised (D)	4·21
Children sent to bed early (H)	4·10
Good, sensible clothing (H)	4·08
Good conversation and correct speech (F)	4·07
Parents stimulate and help children and carry out ideas (C) ..	3·96
Religious faith (E)	3·77
Space to play (G)	3·71
Visits to interesting places and events (F)	3·53
Parents enjoy good health (G)	3·51
Home not overcrowded (G)	3·51
Parents interested in education (A)	3·48
Culturally rich home, 'right' amusements (F)..	3·41
Mother not working (G)	3·16
Family financially secure (G)	3·12
Parents intelligent, educated (C)	2·78
Travel and holidays (F)	2·61
Parents help with school work (A)	2·39

[1] Letters in brackets refer to the groupings of items when the teachers' answers to the open-ended question in the Initial Questionnaire were analysed, e.g. 'A' means this item suggested by a teacher was classified under the heading 'Interest in School Progress'.

A	Interest in School Progress
B	Emotional Climate
C	Motivational
D	Regularity, Organization and Training
E	Moral Training
F	Cultural
G	Economic
H	Material Provision

Comparing the extreme social areas, (middle and lower working) the middle-class area teachers attached significantly more importance to 'parental help with school work', 'a religious faith', 'stable emotional home life', a 'non-working mother'; and to a lesser extent 'parental stimulation', 'intelligence' and 'education'.

School organization, teacher's position or social class origin appeared to be much less important than the factor of the school's social area. For instance, heads and class teachers differed in only one respect; heads attached more importance to the emotional stability of the home. Teachers in junior mixed and infant schools appeared to attach more importance to the 'Interest in School Progress' group of items than teachers working in the larger infant only schools. Examining social class origin within school social areas, it was teachers of middle-class origin in the lower working-class schools who rated parental stimulation and parental health more highly, whilst those of working-class origin attached more importance to firm but kindly discipline in the home. In the other areas, the only difference was in relation to the item on parental financial security; teachers of working-class origin attached more importance to this item.

Two other variables included in the analysis were the school's religious denomination and the teacher's age. (See further details, Appendix D, pages 130-4.) As was to be expected, the teachers in the church schools rated the item concerning a religious faith more highly, but these teachers did not differ significantly from those in non-church schools regarding the rating of the other items in the 'moral training' group. Generally, older teachers tended to attach more importance to the moral training, emotional and economic groups of items.

Findings: 3. Rating Question—Total scores

The teachers' total scores on the rating question were used in several analyses, details of which are reported in Appendix D, (pp. 132-4). Briefly, the results suggested that it was the older, more authoritarian teachers and those with unfavourable attitudes to pupils and their homes who tended to score more highly. If high scores on this question can be interpreted as indicative of an interest in the contribution of the 'good' home, then it would also seem to be logical to expect that such an interest would be related to the teacher's type of personality and age (or experience).

B. Information and 'Clues'

Procedure

The material used for this part of the study was provided by the answers given by the heads and the reception class teachers to the questions in the third part of the *Initial Questionnaire*. Most of the questions were open-ended, but in some places teachers were asked to give their answers in the form of estimates.

Findings: 1. Personal Contacts

Parent-teacher organizations or regular meetings with parents. Only 9 per cent of the schools had parent-teacher organizations, although a further five schools stated they held regular meetings to which parents were invited. Some heads answered that they had found parent-teacher associations difficult to keep going: 'The same parents always come along—we can see them any time. It's the parents we never see that we should like to get along'. One head who had established a flourishing organization, expressed the opinion that its success was due to the fact that it had an extensive social programme which included folk dancing, and the formation of a team of dancers which represented the school in competitions had helped to give the association a corporate identity. This school was in a lower working-class area, and was developing into a lively centre for community activities for the whole neighbourhood.

The objections to the formation of parent-teacher organizations were similar to those reported by Mays (1962)—parents came for the 'wrong' reasons, teachers' anxiety that parents might interfere in the school's organization, and, particularly, teachers' concern that it was the mothers and not the fathers who came to meetings.

No differences in relation to school or teacher variables were statistically significant.

Parents visiting the school. Both the heads and class teachers were asked to estimate the approximate percentage of parents who came to visit them at the school and to describe the reasons for their visits. For the total group, the mean estimate of parents visiting schools was 60 per cent. Reasons for visiting were:

(1) concern related to the child's physical well-being, e.g. absence, health, clothes, undressing for physical education (74 per cent of teachers named such items)

(2)   to make a general inquiry about the child's school progress (63 per cent of teachers)

(3)   to discuss the child's behaviour or parents' anxiety about certain aspects of the child's emotional development

(4)   to ask permission for the child to bring home a reader after a period of absence

(5)   to talk about their own personal troubles

(6)   to complete admission procedures

(7)   to hand in dinner money forgotten by the child or to ask about free meals

(8)   to talk about other children (usually complaints about behaviour towards their own child)

(9)   to thank the teacher or offer help as an expression of gratitude, e.g. bazaars, school events, helping maintain or make equipment

(10) to ask about lost property.

The only differences were related to the teacher variable. Fewer reception class teachers mentioned parents' discussing their personal worries and problems with them or, as might have been expected, coming to see them about admission procedures. However, more parents asked class teachers about lost property, while no head mentioned this as a reason for parents coming to the school. More teachers of working-class origin mentioned that parents visited the school for reasons connected with their children's physical well-being.

Children accompanied to school. The reception class teacher, as the teacher of the youngest children, was expected to be the class teacher most likely to see parents when they brought their children to school and therefore most likely to meet parents regularly in informal circumstances. Reception class teachers were therefore asked to estimate the approximate percentage of pupils who came alone, or were brought to school by parents, siblings, older children or neighbours. The mean estimate of these teachers was that 15 per cent came by themselves, 55 per cent of their pupils were brought by their parents, 19 per cent came with a brother or sister, 6 per cent with another child and 5 per cent came with a neighbour or other parent. It may seem surprising that the only difference in relation to the school's social area was that more teachers in middle- than working-class schools reported pupils coming to school by themselves. This was the impression the reception class teacher received, but some of these children may have been dropped near the school gates by parents with cars, or parents in these areas may have been less likely to accompany their children into the school grounds.

Visiting of pupils' homes by teachers. Both heads and class teachers were asked if they ever visited pupils' homes and, if so, in what circumstances. Only 9 per cent of teachers said they were in the habit of visiting pupils in their homes. A further 18 per cent said they might do so, but only in exceptional circumstances, such as taking a child home after an accident or to visit a child who had been ill for some time. Three out of four teachers answered that they had never been inside the homes of these urban pupils. The teachers who were on visiting terms replied that they were asked to come to pupils' homes on a child's birthday, in order to see a new baby, or for a christening—that is, visits were usually purposeful and generally to mark a particular occasion. As might have been expected, fewer heads than class teachers replied that they never visited pupils' homes.

Findings: 2. 'Clues'

Amount of absenteeism and lateness. The teachers were asked about their pupils' absenteeism and lateness to discover whether such records could indicate to teachers differences in parental attitudes, particularly in relation to the importance and value the parents attached to regular schooling and prompt attendance. Recognized schools are required by the Department of Education and Science regulations to keep attendance registers for each term to show the presence or absence of each pupil who is required by law to be present. Both heads and class teachers were asked to give the mean annual percentage attendance, an estimate based on the weekly recorded percentage attendance. In addition, both heads and class teachers were asked to estimate the amount of absenteeism and lateness by means of a three-point scale.

The mean percentage attendance of pupils based on the recorded attendance figures supplied by heads was 84·34; by reception class teachers 81·74. The lower figure for the reception class teacher is not unexpected, since new entrants have a higher absenteeism figure. They tend to catch childhood complaints, such as measles, in their first year, as they are less likely to have been in contact with contagious illnesses before starting school. The mean percentage attendance for each absence category was as follows: not much absenteeism—85·9 per cent; some absenteeism—82·7 per cent; a lot

35

of absenteeism—75·0 per cent. This would suggest that these teachers' estimates of absenteeism were reliable,[1] and that on the basis of recorded attendance, the teachers who answered that they had 'a lot of absenteeism' did, indeed, have more of a problem in comparison with other schools. No differences proved to be significant in relation to the school and teacher variables.[2]

Reasons for absenteeism and lateness. Sandon (1961) has stated: 'The most commonly accepted reason for absence is sickness, though absence in order to spend holidays with parents is also recognized. In the very great majority of cases, sickness is given as the cause of absence'. In this present study the reasons given by the children for being absent were of the types mentioned by Sandon—illness of child, his parents or family (98 per cent of teachers mentioned this type of reason) or holidays, including those spent in hop-picking by some of the East End children (44 per cent of teachers). Shopping and visits with the parents were mentioned by 23 per cent of teachers, and other reasons cited by the teachers were late nights and subsequent oversleeping by the child, the child being sent on errands and kept away from school, truanting, absence for the purpose of religious observances, the child remaining at home because the mother did not get up in time to see him off to school, or the child being kept at home because of inadequate clothing. The reasons for lateness given by the children were usually that children had to get themselves up as their mothers overslept (these reasons were characterized by the fact that the teacher singled the mother out for blame—40 per cent of teachers mentioned this type of reason), that the children themselves overslept (38 per cent), or that the mother, child or parents were ill, had had an accident, or had had a medical or clinic visit (17 per cent). As many as eight other reasons were given, but none of these were mentioned so frequently.

---

[1] The study of pupils in Scottish primary schools by Morrison, McIntyre and Sutherland (1965) reported that teachers' assessments of objective measures of attendance/absenteeism were independent of their assessments of pupils' other traits.

[2] That school social area differences were not significant is in line with Mays' (1962) suggestion that the majority of parents of the Crown Street school pupils in Liverpool tended to send their children to school regularly and that the problem of poor attendance was 'concentrated on a small minority of families, and it is something that is more characteristic of a family than of individual children'. There is evidence from the National Survey of Health and Development records (Douglas and Ross, 1965) that it is the eldest child in large families who in particular is likely to have many periods of absenteeism during his schooling. On the whole, children often away in the first two years made good attendance in subsequent years and caught up, but not if they came from lower working-class homes or went to primary schools with poor academic records.

It is possible that reasons for absenteeism and lateness such as those which have been described, give teachers insights into their pupils' home lives of which they might otherwise be unaware.

The only difference in types of reasons given for absenteeism was that fewer teachers in infant only schools mentioned shopping with parents; perhaps this is a more 'acceptable' reason in the smaller, junior mixed and infant school. In enumerating excuses for lateness, more heads of infant only schools mentioned 'children dawdling on the way and being reluctant to come to school', whereas more heads of the smaller junior mixed and infant schools reported that children were late because 'they went on errands'. In upper working-class areas more heads mentioned 'family crisis', usually, 'the clock stopped' as a reason for being late, whereas heads in lower working-class areas were more likely to believe it was because the mother was working. Among the class teachers, 'illness' was more frequently mentioned by teachers in the upper working-class areas, and more teachers in the lower working-class schools referred to the mother's employment as the reason for the child's lateness. Finally, in regard to the teacher variables, there was only one difference— more heads than class teachers blamed watching television late at night for tardiness at school next morning.

Indications of pupils' material circumstances. Both heads and reception class teachers were asked whether there were any ways in which they could assess the general living standard or income of their pupils' homes.

Four out of five teachers agreed that there were ways by which they could gain some idea of a child's material circumstances. Half of these teachers mentioned the type and quality of a child's clothing, including whether or not they wore a school uniform when the practice was encouraged in the school. In order of frequency, other 'clues' were said to be:

(1) the child's possessions observed at school
(2) the types of holidays and visits described by children
(3) the amount of pocket money
(4) whether the school photograph was purchased
(5) buying National Savings Stamps at school
(6) children's response to appeals and their gifts for others
(7) whether a child had free dinners or was in receipt of other welfare provision
(8) information (unspecified) gained by talking to parents or children

37

  (9)   information from child's drawings, stories or 'News' period
(10)   child's cleanliness, language, speech, behaviour and manners
(11)   their respect for equipment and property
(12)   their general knowledge and familiarity with books
(13)   their father's job or occupation
(14)   the family's hire purchase commitments
(15)   parental interest in child's activities
(16)   whether family received welfare benefits
(17)   parents' appearance
(18)   whether parents were saving for a home of their own
(19)   whether the mother was working.

Of the teachers who said they were unable to assess the standard of living of their pupils, seventeen did not elaborate in any way, but twelve went on to explain that the child's appearance, toys, etc. were only an indication of *how* the money was spent—not how *much* was coming into the home. Five teachers commented that outward signs such as parental care, appearance of the child, etc. were related to the *character* of the parents and not the money coming into the home. Other reasons given were that in a new housing estate children would tend to come from homes with similar tastes; children today tend to have similar toys and possessions; rents vary considerably and some families might be saving for a house and therefore may have less spending money; whilst in other cases, the family income would be greater if both parents worked.

Among the class teachers, more teachers in middle-class and fewer in lower working-class areas answered that they were *unable* to assess pupils' material circumstances.

Other school and teacher differences were as follows: significantly more heads of the smaller, combined department schools mentioned the type of holiday taken by pupils' families as indicative of income level, and more heads of lower than upper working-class schools mentioned pupils' clothing. Also, more class teachers than heads referred to the importance of clothing. In this connection, it should be pointed out that it is probably the class teacher who supervises pupils' changing for physical education, and although the standard of external clothing may be similar, class teachers commented that it was often the *type and condition of underclothing* which was a 'real clue' in these circumstances. Class teachers supervise dressing at going home time, so provision of gloves and head covering in cold weather were also mentioned as further such 'clues'. In regard to the teacher's social class origin, more teachers of working-class origin considered that the amount and the practice of giving pocket money was indicative of home circumstances.

Needy families. Heads were also asked if they had 'needy' families amongst their pupils and to describe what sort of provision was made for these children, and how they came to their notice. All but 4 per cent of the heads reported they had such children in their schools, and most mentioned the Free Dinner Service or the Care Committee as the main provision for such children. Half of them referred to gifts of clothing, the assistance of the parish or health visitor, the help of the school doctor, or holidays being specially organized for these children. About half the heads who answered that they had such families, added that they were few in number. As one would expect, significantly fewer heads of lower working- than middle-class area schools commented that 'needy' families were infrequent.

Indications of parental interest. Both the heads and class teachers were asked to describe the ways in which parents of pupils were able to show their desire for their children to make progress in learning to read. The most often mentioned way was by making inquiries about their children's progress (42 per cent of teachers). Other indications of parental interest, in order of frequency, were: buying or asking about suitable books (25 per cent), asking how or whether they could help children with their school work (23 per cent) and buying or borrowing the reader in the reading scheme for their child to use at home (21 per cent). Other ways mentioned by the teachers included encouraging children to join a local library, parents attending school Open days, reading aloud to their children and discussing pictures in the books read together, hearing children read aloud, helping with sounds, teaching children the alphabet before they came to school, teaching them to write their own names, showing an interest in the child's school work, praising their efforts, showing pleasure when they gain confidence in using the skill, coming to school after school hours to hear the child read, showing anxiety if progress is not maintained, or asking about the methods in use in the school.

It can be seen from the preceding paragraph that teacher perception of parental interest can take a number of forms. Some teachers may expect parents to show their interest in an active way, as for example, by coming to the school and supporting school events, whereas others will be content if the parent simply praises the child's efforts and provides a background of encouragement and affection. It should be noted that one in five of these teachers commented that *their* pupils' parents rarely or never showed any interest.

School and teacher differences. In regard to school organization, more heads of junior mixed and infant schools referred to parents getting their children to join the local public library and to parents coming to the school to ask about the methods used. However, among the reception class teachers, significantly more infant only teachers expected parents to show an interest in their children's work and to praise their efforts, suggesting that it was the former type of school which expected the more overt display of parental interest. Social area appeared to have two effects: heads of middle-class area schools were more likely to expect parents to buy a copy of the school reader for use at home, whereas more heads in lower working-class schools mentioned the word 'borrow'. Among the class teachers, fewer in upper working-class areas mentioned that parents asked for advice about suitable books for their children.[1]

In regard to the teacher variables, significantly more heads than class teachers felt that parents' interest was evidenced by attendance at Open days, the provision of a copy of the reader for the child's use at home, anxiety if their children did not maintain progress, and willingness to hear their children read aloud at home (the last two items being at a lower level of statistical significance). Finally,

---

[1] In the lower working-class areas the question of advice over reading material assumes importance, because teachers feel that, although parents may have the money to buy books for their children's use, they will not be able to choose the book appropriate to the child's stage of development because of the parents' intellectual inferiority or lack of education.

'They *will* buy Annuals from Woolworths, and then wonder why their child, who is on an Introductory reader, cannot read them!'—Lower working-class area Head.

In these areas, the interested parent is the one who will seek out the teacher and ask for advice—'What sort of book do I buy for his birthday? In middle-class areas, parents are expected to be able to use their judgement and not worry the school with 'trivialities'. In these areas, the interested parent is considered to be the one who will supply a variety of reading material, and not merely duplicate the reading schemes supplied in the classroom.

It is interesting to note in this context that one very real difficulty for parents living in lower working-class areas is the absence of local book shops. One head expressed surprise to the author over the fact that in her school's locality there was no branch of the well-known book shop that she regularly patronized in the middle-class residential suburb where she lived. She considered that it was not surprising that the parents of her pupils lost their initial enthusiasm to provide the 'right' reading material and soon fell back upon buying the commodity sold in the local sweet shop or the nearest chain or self-service store.

more heads of working-class origin referred to the fact that parents borrowed rather than bought a copy of the reader used in the school.

C. Inferences About Occupational Levels

Procedure

The school's social area does not appear to affect teachers' estimates of objective measures of attendance/absenteeism which involve the keeping of records. In this study the teachers were asked to estimate the incidence of certain environmental factors sometimes involving record keeping. The next step, therefore, was to examine these other estimates to see whether they were affected by the social area of the school and how they compared with less subjective measures. The first analysis was concerned with the relationship of the teachers' estimates and an objective economic measure (the J-Index). The findings of this analysis are reported in Appendix D, (pp. 135-6). The second analysis was concerned with the reliability of teachers' estimates of paternal occupations, a form of assessment sometimes used in research as a measure of pupils' social class. For comparative purposes we had two less subjective measures: (a) the percentage distribution of male occupation in the school ward, Census data 1951 (this was the criterion used to assess the social area of the school), and (b) the actual paternal occupations of the 1954 age-group pupils (where the school kept or had access to this information). In eighty cases there were estimates of paternal occupations by the head as well as Census data, and fifty gave all three measures—estimate, Census data and recorded paternal occupation. The findings of this analysis are reported here in some detail, as they have a bearing upon the results of the teachers' general estimates of pupils and their comments, which were asked for in the *Home Background (General)* form.

Findings

As can be seen from Table IV/B, there was a close association between the heads' estimates and pupils' fathers' recorded occupations, but there was also a close relationship between the heads' estimates and the other objective measure—the Census data, which increased when only the schools with records were considered. A close relationship had not been expected between heads' estimates and Census data for three reasons: (1) the Census information dated

TABLE IV/B: Intercorrelations of Three Assessments of Pupils' Social Class—(1) Teachers' Estimates, (2) Social Class Index Based on Census Data, (3) Pupils' Recorded Paternal Occupations.

VARIABLE	N=80		N=50			N=37			
	Estimates	Census Data	Estimates	Census Data	Records	Estimates	Census Data	Records	Soc. Class Origin
Estimates	1·00	*** 0·47	1·00	*** 0·53	*** 0·74	1·00	*** 0·53	*** 0·76	N.S. 0·26
Census Data ..	—	1·00	—	1·00	** 0·43	—	1·00	* 0·38	N.S. 0·21
Records	—	—	—	—	1·00	—	—	1·00	N.S. 0·19
Social Class Origin	—	—	—	—	—	—	—	—	1·00

from 1951 whilst the teachers' estimates were made in 1959 and, during the period that had elapsed, redevelopment schemes and housing policies had tended to change the social composition of particular areas; (2) the Census figures referred to the proportion of occupied males over 15 years of age in different occupations in the ward, and this might not correspond with the percentage of married males with families of school age; (3) school populations may differ in social composition from their immediate neighbourhoods if a school tends to attract pupils from a particular social class because of its reputation.

Over/under-estimation of social class. The next step was to look at the schools with both estimates and records, and to express the difference between the value based on the head's estimate and that based on records as either a positive or negative value. When these plus or minus values were correlated with the Census data (that is, the school social area), the co-efficient was 0·46, large enough to indicate a positive relationship (significant at 1 per cent) between the head's tendency to over- or under-estimate their pupils' social class (or paternal occupations), and the social area of the school. In other words, the higher the social area of the school, the more heads were inclined to estimate their school population as being 'better' than the level of occupations recorded. The implication of this finding would seem to be that teachers' expectations about particular regions and their ideas regarding the likelihood of certain types of employment, are more influential than the actual recorded occupations of pupils' fathers. Did this seem likely? How in practice would it occur? At least three points needed further elaboration:

(1) Were there certain occupations that teachers would have difficulty in classifying, so that, in particular instances where a teacher was doubtful, their assumptions about the predominance of certain types of occupations would take over and the particular occupation would be up- or down-graded to fit in with these assumptions?

(2) What happened when teachers did not have access to or keep records of parents' occupations? Would expectations about areas operate to the same extent, or would another factor—for instance, the teacher's social class origin—assume more importance in these circumstances?

(3) Why did some schools keep records of pupils' paternal occupations, and not others?

43

Recording paternal occupation. Looking first at the relationship between teachers' estimates and their social class origin, there were only thirty-seven cases where the information was complete for all three measures as well as the teacher's social class origin, and in these cases, no significant relationship was found between the teacher's class origin and the three measures. However, when the correlations were based on the maximum number of cases (N=47), the relationship between teachers' estimates and teachers' social class origins reached a low level of significance (5 per cent). This larger group included the eleven schools whose heads did not record pupils' paternal occupations. The social class origin of nine of these heads was known, and a calculation of mean estimates for the two groups, heads of middle- and of working-class origin, showed that the mean for the middle-class group was higher than that for the working-class (1 per cent). When asked to estimate the school population in social class terms, it appears that the teacher without records tends to base his impressions on those pupil characteristics and values familiar to him from his own social background, but more research is necessary before any definite conclusions can be drawn.

Classifying occupations. To return to the question of teachers' ability to classify occupations, in the *Home Background* (*General*) form, teachers were asked to rank a short list of occupations for which the rankings by a representative group of judges was available (Hall-Jones Classification). These teachers showed a similar variability of judgement in the middle ranges of the social scale, so that it seems probable that teachers, like most middle-class professional groups, have least difficulty in classifying occupations in the extreme groups and are familiar with the status differences of their own social group—professional and intermediate occupations. Further, there is evidence which suggests that people of middle-class origin, and those aspiring to the middle-class, tend to use different criteria in judging occupations from those in the working-class.[1] Those with middle-class values tend to stress the power and responsibility which the occupation commands in the community rather than the usefulness of the job. Since authority and responsibility have previously been related to educational opportunity and hence to intellectual ability, it would not be surprising to find that teachers generally associate intellectual ability and occupational level. If this follows, one would expect to find that teachers have less knowledge of the degrees of responsibility involved in manual

[1] See Himmelweit, Halsey and Oppenheim (1952).

44

occupations.[1]   As a consequence, teachers in working-class areas would tend to think of their pupils as homogeneous groups in terms of social class and, therefore also, as homogeneous groups in regard to intellectual ability.   They would expect to find few bright pupils, and indeed, as is reported later in this chapter, this was what occurred —more teachers in the lower working-class areas estimated that they had no pupils of above average intellectual ability.[2]

Homogeneous social groups.   In the *Home Background* (*General*) form both heads and class teachers were asked to complete estimates of pupils' social class on a five-point scale using the categories, 'all', 'most', 'some', 'few', 'none'.   Professional and clerical occupations were grouped and considered as one class (middle); skilled occupations (working), and semi and unskilled (lower working).   When the estimates were examined, comparing those teachers who used only the working-class categories with those who used all the groupings or only the extremes, it was found that more teachers in lower working-class area schools estimated that all their pupils came from manual homes.   However, fewer heads (most of whom had access to records of paternal occupations) estimated that they had only pupils of manually employed fathers in their schools.

[1] In the *Home Background* (*General*) form, the teachers were asked to give typical examples of the different occupational groupings.   These teachers were all sure that a bus conductor was engaged in a manual occupation but they were not agreed about the skill involved in this particular occupation.   The social area of the school appeared to make a difference to the classification of this and similar occupations; teachers in working-class areas classified it as skilled and teachers in middle-class areas gave it as an example often of semi or unskilled occupations.   Also, teachers appeared to have difficulties with what one might term the newer professions and occupations, where they were uninformed about the educational or intellectual concomitant of the job.   For instance, the occupation 'architect' was given as an example in three different classes— professional, clerical and skilled.   Teachers in all three areas cited this occupation as professional, but some teachers in middle-class areas described it as clerical, whilst lower and upper working-class area teachers named it as skilled manual.   This suggests that in some teachers' minds there is confusion as to whether this type of employment is manual by reason of the fact that the architect uses his hands or whether, on the basis of training, education and services rendered, it is considered as professional and therefore non-manual.

[2] This tendency for teachers in lower working-class areas to under-estimate the proportion of bright pupils has also been reported by Crawford in Mays' Liverpool study (1962).   She mentions that teachers in the disadvantaged areas sometimes said that they had 'a very high proportion of dull children to cope with and very few bright ones to compensate for them and to set a high level of attainment for the classes'.   In that study, however, it was found that the range of ability within the disadvantaged area was very wide, just as wide as in other districts of Liverpool, and the measure of ability was the Terman-Merrill Test, which is a highly verbal test.

Teachers' general estimates of pupils. In the same form the teachers were asked to estimate the level of intellectual ability of their pupils, pupils' parental interest in their children's progress and the quality of home background of pupils. As indicated in the above discussion, more teachers in the lower working-class areas replied that they had no pupils of above average intellectual ability. With regard to parental interest and the type of home, more lower working-class area teachers reported that few parents were interested in comparison with the other two areas where more teachers answered that *all* parents were interested. (No teacher used the 'none' category.) More lower working-class area teachers said either few or some pupils came from 'good' homes and fewer of these teachers made use of the 'all' or 'most' categories. Space was provided for the comments of the teachers after each estimate, and a summary of their comments is included in Appendix D (pp. 135-40).

General estimates and over/under-estimation of pupils' social class. Finally, the heads' general estimates of pupils' intelligence and parental interest were correlated with their social class origin, and with their over/under-estimation of pupils' social class. Table D/VIII in Appendix D, (p. 139) shows that over/under-estimation of pupils' social class was significantly associated with estimates of pupils' intelligence but *not* with estimates of parental interest. The relationship between heads' social class origin and their estimate of pupils' intelligence and parental interest was not statistically significant.

Teachers' attitudes. None of these London infant teachers considered that their pupils' intellectual ability was particularly outstanding, and the lower the social area of the school the fewer bright children were they likely to expect. Yet despite this, when they were asked in the same form about the ability of children from 'poor' home backgrounds to learn to read, they were convinced generally that most pupils from 'poor' homes could learn to read. Indeed, there was a sizeable group of teachers who believed that all pupils from socially deprived homes could learn. Although teachers generally tended to believe that the lower the social area of the school the more likely it was that the task of teaching children to learn to read would be the responsibility of the teacher alone, their answers suggested that individual teachers would react differently to the situation and that their attitudes and their approach to the problem would be related to their type of personality and characteristic way of reacting to experience. For instance, assuming that the role of a 'frontiersman' might be to some teachers simply a challenge to their professional expertise, to others, the same situation could be interpreted as a fight for survival in an alien culture. The following contrasting opinions from different teachers both employed in lower working-class area schools illustrates this point:

(a) 'Naturally it is important and desirable to have parents interested; clean, secure, steady homes, moral and spiritual standards, etc. but where this is lacking it is up to the teachers and thus the school to provide the security and standards which children need.'

(b) 'Teaching children in an area such as this, is extremely difficult and *very* tiring.'

References

BERNSTEIN, B. (1960). 'Language and social class', *Brit. J. Sociol.*, XI.

BERNSTEIN, B. (1961). 'Social class and linguistic development: a theory of social learning'. In: FLOUD, J., *et al.*, eds. *Education, Economy and Society*. Glencoe: Free Press.

DOUGLAS, J. W. B. and ROSS, J. M. (1965). 'The effects of absence on primary school performance', *Brit. J. Educ. Psychol.*, XXXV, 1, 28-40.

HALL, J. and CARADOG-JONES, D. (1950). 'The social grading of occupations', *Brit. J. Sociol.*, I, 1.

HIMMELWEIT, H. T., HALSEY, A. H. and OPPENHEIM, A. N. (1952). 'The views of adolescents on some aspects of the social class structure', *Brit. J. Sociol.*, III, 2, 148-72.

INGLIS, W. B. (1948). 'The early stages of reading: a review of recent investigations'. In: *Studies in Reading*, Vol. 1. London: University of London Press.

JACKSON, B. and MARSDEN, D. (1962). *Education and the Working Class*. London: Routledge.

MAYS, J. B. (1962). *Education and the Urban Child*. Liverpool: Liverpool University Press.

MORRISON, A., McINTYRE, D. and SUTHERLAND, J. (1965). 'Teachers' personality ratings of pupils in Scottish primary schools', *Brit. J. Educ. Psychol.*, XXXV, 3, 306-19.

MUSGROVE, F. and TAYLOR, P. H. (1965). 'Teachers' and parents' conception of the teacher's role', *Brit. J. Educ. Psychol.*, XXXV, 2, 171-9.

SANDON, F. (1961). 'Attendance through the school year', *Educ. Res.*, 111, 2, 153-6.

CHAPTER V

Assessments of Individual Pupils

There is a danger of labelling children and expecting good results from a good home and not expecting as much from a child of a poor home. I think it is very useful to know about a child's background, but we should still aim to treat each child as an individual with his own character, interests and intelligence.
(Class teacher, working-class origin, employed
in working-class area school).

PROCEDURE

THE teachers of the 1954 age group of pupils kept four types of records:

(a) Estimates of the characteristics of individual children's home circumstances; (b) estimates of the personality characteristics of each child; (c) estimates for each child of certain factors related to progress in reading; (d) estimates of the reading attainment and progress of each child. [Information pertaining to (a), (b) and (c) was recorded on the *Home Background* (*Individual*) form; information for (d) was on the *Reading Readiness* estimate and *Primer Criterion* form.]

The information available from these records was analysed only in relation to the school variables, social area and organization. It was not possible to examine the material in relation to the two teacher variables, position and social class origin, because not all the teachers had been asked to complete *Personal Questionnaires*. In addition, in those cases where the 1954 age group was taught by more than one teacher, it was not always possible to identify the teacher completing each individual child's estimate.

FINDINGS

(a) *Estimates of individual children's home circumstances.*

The teachers were asked to record for each child the incidence of

ITEM	COMPARISON OF LEVELS OF RESPONSE						COMPARISON OF AFFIRMATIVE/NEGATIVE ANSWERS					
	Percentage of Affirmative and Negative Replies						*Percentage of Affirmative Answers*					
	Total	Infant Only	J.M. & I	Lower Wkg.	Upper Wkg.	Middle Class	Total	Infant Only	J.M. & I	Lower Wkg.	Upper Wkg.	Middle Class
1. Parental help with school work	80·7	79·8	82·2	88·3	73·2	79·4	59·4	58·0	61·7	56·0	58·6	65·2
2. Child familiar with and appreciative of reading	95·3	94·9	96·0	98·4	90·2	97·2	78·7	80·0	76·4	76·8	78·3	81·5
3. Home with well ordered routine	74·9	72·2	79·6	80·6	68·6	74·7	83·8	85·1	81·8	80·0	85·4	87·6
4. Emotionally stable home	75·5	73·1	79·8	81·2	67·4	77·5	83·9	86·6	79·7	80·1	86·9	86·1
5. Mother not working or, if she does, makes provision	88·4	87·9	89·4	92·7	84·0	88·1	94·2	95·3	92·4	93·0	93·5	96·7
6. Child seems to get enough sleep	96·0	96·1	95·8	98·5	93·9	95·0	81·3	81·6	80·9	75·8	85·2	84·5
7. Satisfactory housing conditions	68·8	68·0	70·1	68·9	61·3	77·2	89·0	91·9	84·2	85·9	87·2	94·2
8. Parental interest in child's school progress	88·5	87·9	89·5	93·1	84·3	87·5	72·6	71·6	74·2	66·4	75·1	78·4
9. Child's television watching planned, supervised	36·8	29·4	49·8	47·0	27·4	34·4	59·7	66·5	52·7	48·6	62·1	77·2
10. Parents take an interest in child's activities	74·7	71·9	79·4	80·5	66·4	76·7	82·8	83·9	81·7	79·9	83·6	85·9

C

ten attributes related to pupils' home conditions.[1] The numbers of affirmative and negative answers for the various children making up the different school organization and social area groupings were expressed as percentages of all children in the group. The percentages for all children, and the comparisons of affimative and negative answers and levels of response are shown in Table V/A—'Teachers' Knowledge of Individual Pupils' Home Background'.

One or two comments need to be made about the teachers' answers. Although parental help with school work had not been ranked highly as characteristic of the 'good' home, the teachers claimed, on the basis of their records, that more than half their pupils had this type of help. It should be remembered that these pupils were six-year-olds who would not have homework in any real sense of the word, but who could only receive help from their parents in the form of assistance with the practice of the basic skills, e.g. being 'heard' to read aloud.

The highest proportion of affirmative answers was in relation to mother not working, or making provision if she did. There were very few children whom teachers were prepared to identify as 'latch-key' children. Nevertheless, in conversation with teachers, particularly those employed in the lower working-class area schools, this absence of the mother from home was often suggested as being both a detrimental factor and a common practice. The lowest proportions of affirmative answers were in relation to whether parents helped with school work and whether television watching was supervised. In relation to parental help, teachers' negative answers could have two meanings: either that the teachers did not expect parental help because the children were too young for homework, or that the teachers considered the parents did not help in the ways which were open to them. The item on television watching was intended as a check question. Because teachers' observations would be very limited, the obvious answer for most children would be 'no information'. Teachers might interpret indirect evidence such as comments about programmes in the 'News' period, as indications of whether television watching was supervised, but generally this item was expected to produce the least

---

[1] In the *Home Background (General)* form these items (with one exception—parental help with school work) had been rated by the teachers as of considerable importance to the learning situation. Heads had attached slightly more importance to the item regarding the emotional stability of the home, and there had been social area differences in relation to three of the items (help with school work, working mothers, stable homes), but the teachers had been generally agreed about the relative importance of the other seven items.

amount of information, which was what occurred. The two items which gave teachers the least trouble were those concerned with the adequacy of sleep and familiarity with reading material. In both instances, teachers would be able to draw inferences; for example, a child might fall asleep in class, or be unsure of how to turn the pages of a book, or treat reading material with lack of care.

Differences. Two components were distinguished in the teachers' assessments: the level of response (the percentage of teachers making a reply whether affimative or negative), and the proportion of affirmative to negative replies. Differences were examined for all ten items in relation to (a) social area, (b) organization, and (c) organization within social area. Further details, including two tables of results, are given in Appendix E (pp. 141-4).

Briefly, the findings were that there was a very significant association between the teachers' rating of individual pupils' home background and social area for all items. When the two components were separated out, it was clear that level of response was associated with social area. Teachers in the upper working-class areas were more reluctant to rate their pupils on all items. There was also a tendency for rather more teachers in lower working-class areas to make assessments than those in middle-class areas. From the replies of teachers who were able to assess pupils, a consistent pattern emerged. Relatively fewer affirmative answers were given by the teachers in lower working-class areas, whilst teachers in middle-class areas tended to make more positive ratings.

It would seem that teachers in the extreme areas had the most definite ideas about the type of home conditions to be expected. Type of school organization tended to have little effect upon these stereotypes, particularly in the lower working-class areas. However, among those teachers able or willing to assess pupils, infant only teachers generally tended to be less critical in their answers, returning more affirmative answers in relation to their pupils. However, where stereotyped expectations were less in evidence, i.e. in the upper working-class areas, it was the teachers in the infant only schools who were more reluctant to assess pupils. When they did so, they tended to be more critical than the teachers in the combined department schools.

(b) Estimates of individual pupils' personality characteristics.
Differences. The teachers used a checklist of 14 adjectives to record a description of each child's personality. Although teachers in

all social areas reported similar proportions of 'happy', 'naughty' and 'apathetic' pupils, there were significant differences in relation to social area in respect to some of the other attributes. For instance, more children in lower working-class schools were described as 'talkative', 'generous', 'humorous', 'enterprising' (0·1% level of significance) or 'lazy' (5%). In upper working-class areas more pupils were described as 'undersized' (5%), and fewer as 'generous', 'enterprising' (0·1%) or 'lazy' (5%). In middle-class areas fewer pupils were termed as 'undersized', 'lazy' (5%), or 'humorous' (0·1%).[1]

In the light of previous research, it had been expected that the attributes ascribed to pupils in middle-class area schools would tend to be those associated with scholastic progress, and the ethos of the higher social classes. In fact, the findings of this study show that markedly more middle-class area pupils were described by their teachers as 'quiet', 'serious' and 'hard working' pupils. It should be mentioned, however, that these attributes may not be considered entirely desirable in the eyes of the active infant teacher who wishes to encourage co-operative efforts rather than a competitive class spirit.

As regards school organization differences, a significantly higher percentage of pupils in infant only schools were described as 'generous', 'polite', 'humorous', 'healthy', 'happy', 'talkative' (1%) or 'undersized' (5%), whereas more pupils in the junior mixed and infant schools were described as 'dirty' and 'untidy' (5%). Differences in relation to the other seven adjectives were not statistically significant.

It is interesting that the infant only schools differed in relation to five of the seven positive attributes, and probably to a number of infant teachers, 'talkativeness' would be viewed as more a virtue than a vice. Certainly these differences give the impression that the teachers in the infant only school, which tends to be a larger type of organization with children of a two-year range under a head responsible for that age group only, find their pupils more satisfactory

---

[1] Douglas (1964) reported that teachers were reluctant to give an unfavourable opinion when they were asked to assign ten-year-old pupils to one of five categories which varied from 'very hard working' to 'lazy'. The teachers in that study estimated 17 per cent of pupils as working less hard than the average pupil, and very few were prepared to categorize a pupil as 'lazy'. Douglas reported social class differences; a high proportion of the 'hard workers' came from middle-class homes. In the present study, 23 per cent of five-year-olds were rated as 'lazy' by their teachers. Social area differences were significant, more pupils in lower working-class schools being thus described.

and rewarding to teach than do the teachers in the infant department of the combined department primary school. The more positive approach that teachers in infant only schools seem to have towards their pupils might be considered as a relevant factor when comparisons of attainment levels of the two types of school are being made.

(c)   Estimates of factors relevant to pupils' reading achievement

These factors were the child's absenteeism, liking of school, quality of home background, intellectual ability, tendency towards over- or under-achievement, and parents' interest. Table E/II in Appendix E, (p. 144) shows the mean indices for each of these six factors in relation to the group, the school organization and the social area.

Differences.   There were significant differences in relation to social area for the teachers' estimates of pupils' attitude to school, the quality of home background, and parental interest.   Somewhat surprisingly, in the light of previous research, more lower working-class area pupils were said to be fond of school $(0\cdot1\%)$; fewer of these pupils were rated as resenting school and more as liking school very much.   Fewer upper working-class area pupils were rated as liking school on the whole (the middle category in the three-point scale used); and fewer middle-class pupils were rated as liking school very much—in fact, more were said to resent it.

On home background, fewer lower working-class area pupils and more middle-class area pupils were rated as coming from 'good' homes.   However, as with the estimates of the various home factors, teachers in the upper working-class area schools were more reluctant to assess their pupils in relation to quality of home background $(0\cdot1\%)$.   More parents in middle- than lower working-class areas were rated as very interested and frequent visitors to the school $(0\cdot1\%)$.

Of the differences which proved to be non-significant, probably the most unexpected finding was that concerning pupils' intellectual ability.   On the basis of the general estimates, more teachers in lower working-class areas had recorded that they had no pupils of above average intellectual ability; however, when they completed records for individual pupils, social area differences were no longer evident.   One possible explanation might be that when the lower working-class area teachers assessed their pupils individually, they tended to lower their standards regarding what they thought of as 'average' ability, and to accept a lower level of ability in the light of their professional or general expectations about these pupils.

Five of the six factors showed significant differences in relation to school organization; only differences in relation to estimates of pupils' intellectual ability proved to be non-significant. The findings were that the infant only schools appeared to have a slightly better attendance performance (5%)[1] and more pupils in infant only schools were said by their teachers to enjoy school (5%). There was no difference between the incidence of 'good' and 'poor' home ratings, but more teachers in infant only schools were reluctant to rate pupils in relation to this particular factor (0·1%). Also, parents in infant only schools were rated as less interested and were said to visit the school less frequently than the parents of pupils in the junior mixed and infant schools (1%). In the infant only schools there was a smaller estimated range of ability, in that fewer pupils were estimated as doing better or worse in reading 'than expected' and more were rated as doing 'much as one would expect' (the middle category in the three-point scale used).

(d) Estimates of pupils' reading readiness and progress

Teachers recorded their pupils' reading readiness twice during their infant schooling, and these estimates covered four areas: pupils' attitudes to reading activities; their intellectual abilities; development of perceptual abilities; and word recognition skills. School social area and organization differences were found for a number of items, and the findings are reported in detail in Appendix E (pp. 145-8). Table V/B shows the percentage of children attaining each of the various reading readiness items during the first and second years of schooling.

Differences. A number of differences were apparent in relation to social area in the teachers' estimates of pupils' readiness, but a systematic examination suggests that one of two things happened— either the upper working-class pupils were, for some reason,

---

[1] We know from the *Initial Questionnaire* analysis that fewer teachers in the infant only schools mentioned shopping with parents as a reason for absence, so possibly infant only teachers tended to expect a higher standard of attendance, and were less likely to accept any but the 'official' reasons for absence, such as illness or holidays. However, the differences are at a low level of statistical significance—whether they are educationally significant is another matter. In the light of the other findings reported in this research, it would be in keeping to find differences between the two types of organization in relation to standards of attendance, but further research would be necessary to establish whether or not they were in the direction indicated.

TABLE V/B: *Percentage of Children Attaining Each Reading Readiness Characteristic (First and Second Years)*

READING READINESS CHARACTERISTICS	PERCENTAGE OF PUPILS	
	First Year	*Second Year*
(1) Attitude to Reading Activities		
i. interested in all kinds of books ..	65	67
ii. keen to read	61	78
iii. interested in printed word generally ..	49	62
iv. interested in pre-reading activities and materials	69	77
v. interested in stories from books	84	87
(2) Intellectual Ability		
i. sufficient ability to tackle work confidently ..	59	60
ii. good powers of observation and range of ideas	44	47
iii. can think clearly and independently ..	49	52
iv. learns quickly and has good memory ..	44	45
v. capable of understanding own and others' mistakes	46	59
(3) First Stage Perceptual Abilities		
i. can discriminate shapes of letters and words ..	60	84
ii. knows letter names	21	65
iii. can make auditory discriminations	48	74
iv. knows letter sounds	30	63
v. can discriminate shapes generally	72	84
vi. recognizes captions to pictures and objects ..	57	78
vii. associates pattern of words with pictures and ideas	46	72
viii. is aware of left-to-right sequence..	74	94
(4) Second Stage Perceptual Abilities		
i. recognizes classroom words generally ..	59	79
ii. recognizes words out of context..	38	64
iii. recognizes words from introductory readers ..	52	88
iv. recognizes own name	87	97

introduced to systematic reading instruction earlier than were pupils in the other areas (a factor which would give them an initial and continuing advantage), or the teachers of these pupils lowered their standards. The evidence is inconclusive, but possibly the explanation for the apparent comparative superiority of the upper working-class pupils may be found in terms of teachers' standards as reflected by their expectations of pupils' abilities. Teachers of the working-class area pupils (both upper and lower groups) may tend to lower their standards, whereas teachers of middle-class area pupils may be inclined to raise theirs.

Pupils' reading *progress* was assessed in two ways: on the basis of the teacher's record of the pupil's progress through the school reading scheme, and the teacher's estimate (using a three-point scale) of children's progress in reading throughout the year. The book levels reported for pupils from lower working-class areas were significantly lower than those reported for pupils from the other two areas. By the end of the second year, the difference between the two working-class area groups was less marked, but unchanged in relation to the extreme groups. As in the first year, the difference between working- and middle-class area pupils was not significant. As to the teachers' estimates of pupils' progress, by the end of the first year there was a significant difference between the two working-class groups, which was still evident at the end of their infant schooling.

The teachers were asked to predict the type of reader the pupil would become by the age of seven, i.e. the time of transfer or completion of infant schooling. Predictions were made six weeks after the child started school, and again twelve months later—half-way through the first term of the second year. No differences were significant at the start of the pupils' schooling, but by the beginning of the second year differences had appeared. Teachers' predictions for both the middle-class and upper working-class groups were superior to those for the lower working-class group.

When we consider differences in relation to school organization, a somewhat different picture emerges. The results of the teachers' reading-readiness estimates suggest that the two types of schools may have been approaching the teaching of reading in different ways. The junior mixed and infant schools appeared to adopt a more formal approach, in the sense that hardly any settling-in period was allowed, and synthetic methods (particularly systematic phonic teaching) were stressed, so that these pupils were estimated as having more knowledge of the letter names and sounds.[1] However, this early start appeared to result in some loss of interest on the part of these pupils, whilst the infant only schools' tactics of delayed instruction seemed to the teachers in those schools to produce a higher proportion of keen and enthusiastic readers who, by the second year, had a firm foundation of experience and practice, evidenced by their marked superiority in all aspects of perceptual development—except for letter sounds. Pupils in the junior mixed

---

[1] More teachers in junior mixed and infant schools used systematic phonic instruction with all or some pupils in the Reception Class. See Goodacre, 1967 (Report No. 1, chapter VI).

and infant schools, with their early phonic training, were noticeably superior in their knowledge of, and probably also their familiarity with, the sounds of the letters.

It is possible that the difference in approach produced superiority in different aspects of the reading skill, the pupils in the junior mixed and infant schools being better at word recognition, but possibly, as a result, being in danger of 'barking' at print; whereas those in infant only schools had a greater superiority in relation to reading for meaning but may have been held back by their inability to try new words, since they were less familiar with phonics (e.g. recognition of classroom words was significantly higher than recognition of words out of context).

In relation to *progress*, as measured by the book level criterion, the junior mixed and infant pupils showed a slight superiority at the end of the first year, but this had disappeared by the second year, and teachers' estimates of pupils' *progress* showed no significant differences for either the first or second year.

During the first year there was a significant but not large difference between the two types of school, with the pupils in the infant only schools having the more favourable index of *prediction*. By the second year the difference had disappeared.

The evidence from the teachers' predictions of pupils' success would seem to suggest that the approach of the time for transfer to the junior stage may affect the standards of assessment applied by the teachers and that possibly at that level, and from then on, there is more chance of teachers applying uniform criteria. However, by that stage in the primary school, teachers' diverging standards (i.e. their tendency to raise or lower their standards in the light of their expectations of pupils' abilities) may have influenced those differences in the pupils' rates of progress, which, in turn, affect teachers' views of pupils' capabilities.

References

Douglas, J. W. B. (1964). *The Home and the School.* London: MacGibbon & Kee.
Goodacre, E. J. (1967). *Reading in Infant Classes.* Slough: NFER.

C*

CHAPTER VI

Teachers' Attitudes and Personalities

*There is no doubt that many teachers are ignorant of the accepted mores of
the neighbourhood from which many of their pupils come; that many teachers
are, consciously or unconsciously, uncompromisingly hostile to these more
alien 'cultures', and that either attitude handicaps them in their work as
educators (as distinct from instructors). But such attitudes are much less
important in the educative process than those other attitudes we have already
described: attitudes towards children as individuals . . Those of us with
experience in teacher-training find little correlation between socio-political
attitudes or social class on the one hand and progressive educational methods
on the other. What seems to matter far more is the personality of the teacher,
and his ability to initiate warm and friendly relations with other people.*[1]

Procedure

THE questions in the *Personal Questionnaire* were used to obtain
information, firstly, about infant teachers and, secondly, to
discover to what extent teachers within different social areas and
schools of different types of organization differed from the observed
pattern. The information obtained provided some indication of
the personality and character of these teachers; their age; marital
status; education, training and experience; their interest in
reading for enjoyment; their leisure activities and pastimes;
teaching preferences; their descriptions of themselves; and their
satisfactions and frustrations in relation to their occupation.
Altogether, 148 teachers completed the forms: 51 heads and 97 class
teachers. All the heads of the schools taking part in the second
year of the research were approached, and all infant staff in the group
of 34 schools which had been selected as representative of the total
group of schools in relation to school type of organization and
social area. The average return was 75 per cent for heads (total
sample schools) and 76 per cent for class teachers (34 selected
schools).

In this chapter, the findings concerning these infant teachers are
reported for the group as a whole, followed by an account of the
differences in relation to the school and teacher variables, where
these were found to be significant. (The heads were excluded from

[1] WISEMAN, S. (1964). *Education and Environment.* Manchester: University
of Manchester Press.

the analysis when the effects of school organization and area were examined, and social class origin was analysed within social area.) The next section discusses the teachers' attitudes to pupils' home backgrounds, and the chapter concludes with an examination and discussion of the relationship between the heads' personality and attitudes and the level of *school* reading attainment. The way in which the attitude scale was devised, the selection of items and the analysis of the attitudinal factors in relation to those social and psychological factors for which information was obtainable from the *Personal Questionnaire*, are all reported in considerable detail in Appendix F (pp. 155-63).

Findings: (a) *Infant teachers' personal information*

Age. As might have been expected, more heads were older teachers, but none of the differences in relation to the other three variables were significant. Table F/I in Appendix F (p. 151) shows the age distribution for the total and within the groups of teachers.

Marital status. In the total group of heads and class teachers, 56 per cent were single, 32 per cent were married and 12 per cent widowed or divorced. Table F/II in Appendix F (p. 152) shows the number in each category.

Sex. In the total group there were only 14 male teachers, all of whom were heads. Since only the class teachers' answers were used in the analysis in relation to school area and organization and teacher's social class origin, the sex factor was controlled. When the male and female heads' answers were compared, differences in relation to the three variables were not significant.

Place of birth. It was found that 46 per cent of the total group were London-born, 48 per cent from other parts of the British Isles and 6 per cent from overseas. In each social area there were similar proportions of London-born and provincial teachers.[1] Table F/III in Appendix F (p. 152) shows the numbers of teachers in each category in the total and in the groups of teachers.

---

[1] This suggests that in the lower working-class schools, some teachers—possibly the provincial teachers of middle-class origin—would be likely to experience considerable difficulty in understanding pupils' language and local mores unless they had had extensive experience of teaching in these areas. As Inglis has pointed out in *Studies in Reading*, Vol. 1 (1948): 'The child who is to be trained in an approved phonic system may find the sound value which he habitually gives to a letter or combination of letters is very different from that employed by the teacher'.

Social class origin. The teachers were asked to record their parents' occupations; that of their father, and of their mother before and after marriage. Paternal occupation was classified in two ways: using (a) the Registrar-General's five groups, and (b) the Hall-Jones groupings (1950); the correlation between the two types of classification was 0·77 (N=97 class teachers). Using the Registrar-General's groupings 49 per cent of these teachers were of middle-class origin; their fathers had held non-manual jobs. Only sixteen (11 per cent) of the teachers' mothers had worked after marriage, and of these seven had been employed as teachers.

Education, training and experience. Some of this information which was relevant to the first report (Goodacre, 1967) was included in Chapter V dealing with differences in staffing conditions in the schools in different areas. Of the total group, 86 per cent of teachers had received elementary and secondary education and had completed a two- or three-year training course. In addition, 14 per cent of this group had completed a further professional course of at least a year's duration and/or a university degree course. Ten teachers (7 per cent) were 'emergency trained', which meant that, in comparison with the majority of teachers, they had only one year's vocational training instead of two or three. Only six teachers (4 per cent) had received no specialized training. Four teachers were university graduates with no training (3 per cent). Of the total group, 73 per cent were trained to teach infants and 59 per cent had had more than five years' experience of this type of teaching.

As was to be expected, more heads were in the group with additional professional qualifications. However, significantly more class teachers than heads were trained to teach infants, and had more than one year's experience of teaching infants; so that the heads were generally less likely to have had training or experience in relation to teaching young children. More teachers in infant only schools had had less than one year's experience of infant work (or more than twenty years) which suggests that, although the infant only type of schools may have more inexperienced teachers, this is compensated for by the fact that they also have more teachers with many years' experience of teaching infants. As might have been anticipated, heads had been teaching much longer than class teachers. (See Table F/IV in Appendix F (p. 153). As to the length of time the teacher had been in his present post, the tendency was for significantly more class teachers to have been a comparatively short time (0-5 years) compared with heads who had been a moderately long time (6-10 years).   It should be noted that school social area[1] or organization differences were not significant for teachers' length of service in present post.   Table F/V in Appendix F (p. 153) shows the number of teachers in each category for the different variables.

Residence in the school area.   Only one in three of all heads and staff lived in the same borough as that in which their school was situated.   When the teachers were asked to explain their reasons for applying for a post in the particular area, more teachers in the upper working- and middle-class areas answered that they had done so because they were living in the same area as the school for which they had applied.   More class teachers, and teachers in junior mixed and infant schools, had been directed to the post, or had been offered it when they applied to the local education division, whilst more teachers in junior mixed and infant schools had applied for the particular post because it gave them a chance to extend their experience.   Significantly more teachers in infant only schools had applied for their posts because the journey was easier.   Numbers in the middle- and working-class origin groups were too small to test for significant differences in relation to teachers' social class origin.

Reading habits.   The teachers were asked whether they read a daily paper or papers, Sunday paper(s), journals or magazines regularly to find out something about the amount of light reading they did and the types of interests they had, as indicated by the different journals and magazines to which they subscribed.   Also, later in the research, their choice of newspapers, etc. was used as an index of their political sympathies.[2]   The mean total number of

[1] Mays (1962) reported that 40·9 per cent of the school staffs had worked in the Crown Street (Liverpool) schools for a period of five years or more, and he commented that his findings 'help correct the idea that teachers in such schools are constantly on the move and that no stability whatsoever is to be found'.   In the present research, of the London group of teachers, 23 per cent of the lower working-class area teachers had been more than five years in their present post, and in the upper working- and middle-class areas the proportions were similar. Heads were included in Mays' figures, whereas in the present research the London teachers were class teachers only.   'The 1964 National Survey: Data from the Schools', Appendix 5 (Department of Education and Science, 1967) reported that only 35 per cent of the women teachers in infant schools were in the schools to which they had been appointed two years nine months earlier.
[2] The author classified the daily and Sunday papers on the basis of information available from newspaper readership surveys, high values being indicative of left-wing sympathies, low of right-wing or conservative attitudes.   The mean score for all teachers was 11·70; maximum score possible 20; range of scores 6—19; school and teacher differences non-significant.

Sunday, weekly papers and journals read by these teachers was 4·65; range 0-9+; no significant differences between groups were found.

The mean number of interests shown by type of magazine or journal read was 1·98; range 1-5. There was a group of twenty-seven teachers who answered that they did not read any magazine or journal regularly. A number of different interests were represented in the choice of magazines and journals regularly read. Most frequently mentioned publications were vocational ones, closely followed by well known women's publications. Only small groups of teachers (15-17 per cent) regularly subscribed to church, literary, current affairs or gardening publications. Very few mentioned local papers or those publications catering for the interests of specialists, e.g. photography, theatre, etc. although a number of teachers mentioned such interests later in the questionnaire.

Although four out of five teachers subscribed regularly to some magazine or journal, fewer than half of these were likely to choose a vocational publication, and of those who did, only one in three regularly read more than one such paper or journal.[1]

Leisure activities. Teachers were asked to rank nine passive leisure activities: radio listening, newspaper reading, magazine reading, book reading, watching sports, listening to music, watching films, television or theatre.

The reading of books was ranked number one by 49 per cent of the group, followed by listening to music (16 per cent), newspaper reading (14 per cent), and listening to the radio (9 per cent). The activity considered least important by the majority of these teachers, mostly women, was watching sport (53 per cent). One in four named television or films as the activity they enjoyed least. There was no difference between groups in relation to the most popular activity, but it is of some interest that television was not very popular and more teachers in the lower working-class areas or the junior mixed and infant schools recorded this as the item of least importance to them.

---

[1] Johnson (1966) has drawn attention to the need for more inquiry or research into teachers' reading of books and periodicals, especially in regard to their professional reading. Birch (1963) concluded that the majority of teachers did not read much professional literature, suggesting that the major reasons were to be found in their professional training and their attitudes. He believed that many teachers, as first-generation professional people, tended to cling to the characteristic working-class attitude towards work as being the concern of their employer; the idea of continuing their own vocational development by studying and reading after working hours was quite foreign to them. In the present study, 51 per cent of the group could be classed as Birch's first generation professionals.

The teachers were asked also to describe, in order of importance, other leisure activities they enjoyed. The mean number of additional interests named by the total group was 4·16; range 0-8. Although a great number of activities were mentioned, it was possible to group them broadly into seven types: performing a physical skill or sport, professional or civic interests, making something, collecting, gregarious interests (e.g. meeting people, entertaining), musical interests and other activities such as studying, religious duties and politics. One in three of these teachers enjoyed the sort of creative activity which offered a complete relaxation from their daily employment; often the pursuit was one which could best be enjoyed in solitude. The important characteristic of this type of interest seemed to be the production of a finished article, such as a painting, a coffee table, or the re-upholstering of a chair. These tasks produced a compensatory effect in that their creative efforts reached fruition, in contrast to infant teaching where the two-year course is providing so little time in which to see discernible signs of development, to achieve measurable results. Since the school day tends to make many varied demands upon the infant teacher, it was not surprising to find that the solitary nature of particular activities was part of their appeal to some teachers. However, there were some who considered that working with children limited their social contacts, and they tended deliberately to seek adult companionship in their spare time. For these teachers, sport appeared to have little attraction, and none of them mentioned participation in team games. Indeed, when they mentioned taking part in group activities in the community in which they lived, it was noticeable that it was often in a leadership role, e.g. drama producer, choral conductor. Comparatively few of these teachers mentioned activities of a social service or political nature. Undoubtedly domestic responsibilities limited the extent and the types of activities available to many; but even so, the impression was given that even in their own local neighbourhoods these teachers rarely took an active part in the activities of the community, preferring solitary pastimes for their means of 'recreation' and relaxation.

Teaching preferences. The teachers were asked about the type of child they most liked to teach, the form of teaching they most preferred and the type of planning which most appealed to them. The majority of them preferred teaching children of widely varying abilities, since this was a situation which called forth all their teaching talents, and at the same time provided variety in the day-to-day problems encountered. However, one in four would have been happier teaching only bright pupils; another sizeable group preferred teaching a class consisting entirely of pupils of average ability, and five teachers wanted to teach only slow or retarded pupils.

The teachers were almost equally divided in their opinions about the best form of teaching or type of planning. Only ten teachers preferred class teaching—most liked group or individual instruction best. Four teachers preferred a planned scheme, whilst most liked day-to-day planning or following a modified scheme. Only one considered that no scheme at all was preferable.

Self-image. Asked to give a description of themselves, the teachers had to choose from six groups (each consisting of four personality traits), the trait in each group which they considered to be their major strength or weakness respectively. As Table F/VI, Appendix F, (p. 154) shows, most of these infant teachers were in agreement that their best qualities were their cheerfulness, conscientiousness, commonsense and adaptability; and that their weaknesses were their lack of originality, foresight, confidence and ambition. The stereotype of the infant teacher that thus emerges is one of a well-intentioned, somewhat motherly personality anxious about the value of her role in the educational system.

As was to be expected, significantly more heads than class teachers considered leadership to be one of their strong traits. More heads also rated refinement a weakness.

Satisfactions and dissatisfactions. The teachers were asked to select from a list of 17 items those aspects of teaching which they found particularly satisfying, placing the number one against the item giving the most satisfaction. They were also asked to repeat the same procedure in relation to those aspects which they felt to be unsatisfying. As can be seen from Table F/VII, Appendix F, (p. 155) two aspects in particular had great appeal for these infant teachers: (1) the job offered the opportunity to be with children, and (2) it was a worthwhile occupation—a vocation. (Nine out of ten teachers mentioned both of these aspects.) Three out of four teachers mentioned the lengthy holidays, and more than half the group agreed that congenial colleagues, the contacts with parents, the 'responsibility' of the job (probably in the sense of its authority), the independence of action, the hours of work, the opportunities for self expression, the day-to-day variety and the chance to put personal ideals into practice, were the satisfying aspects of this type of teaching.

For two out of three teachers the major satisfaction was either working with children or the vocational aspect. For the rest, the major satisfactions were independence of action, the variety, the chances for putting ideals into practice, the holidays, the opportunities for self-expression, the contacts with parents or colleagues, the hours of work, and the social service opportunities.

More teachers in lower working-class areas were found to be satisfied with the opportunities for independent action, suggesting that these teachers probably experience less anxiety about maintaining standards, and that the absence of parental pressure for high academic standards was interpreted as freedom to experiment in teaching methods, curriculum, etc. More teachers in junior mixed and infant schools were satisfied with their general surroundings.

Significantly more heads were satisfied with the opportunities their job offered for intellectual growth, parental contacts and putting personal ideals into practice.

That a high level of professional satisfaction was expressed by these infant teachers is indicated by the fact that 30 per cent recorded eleven or more satisfactions, 65 per cent four to ten, and only 5 per cent as few as one to three satisfactions. Conversely, 26 per cent recorded *no* dissatisfactions, 53 per cent one to three, and 21 per cent four to ten.[1]

[1] The high level of professional satisfaction of these infant teachers is in accordance with the findings of the study by Rudd and Wiseman (1962) who reported that 'in spite of having to face frustrating classroom conditions infant teachers were particularly satisfied'. They speculated that a possible reason for the high degree of satisfaction expressed by infant teachers was the fact that this group had exceptionally low scores in connection with poor human relations in school, and that it was possible that this, coupled with the satisfactions of the pupil-teacher relationship in such schools, more than offset the difficulties of organization. This view is supported by the present study. A very high proportion of teachers gained satisfaction from working with children, and more than half were satisfied with their relationships with colleagues and parents. However, there is little evidence to support the suggestion of Rudd and Wiseman that women teachers generally tend to be more preoccupied with day-to-day classroom problems rather than being concerned with frustrations in a wider context.

Indeed, if the answers of the classroom teachers are analysed and studied in relation to women teachers only, the two major sources of dissatisfaction are still the lack of intellectual growth afforded by infant teaching and the professional status of the infant teacher. Rudd and Wiseman suggested that 'above all, the irritations reported by this group of subjects made clear that feelings of dissatisfaction would not have been banished by increased public expenditure on salaries, buildings or reducing the size of class'. The present research indicates that the relationship with parents could be improved if heads allowed or encouraged staff to make contacts with parents. This action might help to lessen some of the resentment felt by class teachers, particularly in respect to the loneliness and frustration engendered by teaching infants—'gossip' with parents can help a teacher to learn of the progress made by pupils who have left the in ant school; parental contacts can educate the teacher in the mores of the local community.

The item most often mentioned as a source of dissatisfaction was the *position ascribed to teachers by the community*. Of the teachers who recorded a major dissatisfaction, one in three mentioned this item, although 20 per cent considered the lack of opportunities for intellectual growth the worst aspect. Other major dissatisfactions were the general environment, few chances of promotion, unsatisfactory relationships with parents or with colleagues, and lack of opportunities for independent action, self-expression, idealism or social service. The two items on which teachers did not hold strong opinions or to which they had given little thought (that is, the items with the highest 'no opinion' ratings) were (1) the somewhat ambiguously worded item on opportunities for social service (49 per cent of teachers) and (2) the item referring to *promotion chances* (43 per cent).

More teachers in upper working- and middle-class areas were dissatisfied with the opportunities for independent action, thus providing further evidence of the tendency for teachers in the higher social areas to view parental expectations as a restriction on their freedom to experiment and introduce innovations. More teachers in the infant only schools were dissatisfied with their surroundings [despite the fact that these schools tended to be larger and less restricted regarding space and storage facilities (Goodacre, 1967)]. Perhaps the teachers in the infant only schools had higher standards in regard to material conditions than their colleagues in the combined department schools, who were generally more satisfied about being able to put their personal ideals into practice.

Class teachers were generally slightly less satisfied than heads, particularly in regard to the opportunities their work offered for intellectual growth, independence of action, putting ideals into practice, and the contacts with parents.

The infant teacher image. The teaching preferences, self ratings and job satisfaction answers of this group of teachers provide some evidence of how infant teachers tend to see themselves within the educational system. They appear to be uncertain of their professional worth, show signs of insecurity and awareness of lack of vocational ambition which may be related more to domestic responsibilities and social background, than to the level of their general ability. However, despite this sense of insecurity, they expressed a high degree of satisfaction in their occupation. This satisfaction appeared to be related to their appreciation of the pupil-teacher relationship and the positive pleasure these women teachers experience through the sublimation of maternal feelings through socially acceptable channels. Obviously, this type of teaching satisfies emotional needs, but anxiety may arise when the teacher becomes aware of her status within the educational system. The absence of intellectual stimulation in comparison with other types of teaching may become a cause of major dissatisfaction when responsibilities and home commitments are such as to prevent the development of the teacher's own interests or studies. However, these teachers seem diffident about attempting the more 'vocational' types of interests, possibly, as Birch has suggested, because a higher proportion of these teachers are first-generation professionals and may in fact be quite content with their enjoyment of 'women's interests'. At times, however, they may experience guilt about their lack of ambition and professional drive which they feel they *ought* to have. If this group of infant teachers is typical of teachers at this level of the educational system, an important and characteristic personal quality may be their inability to express themselves convincingly and logically in relation to the needs of their sector of the educational system. Those employed at the tertiary level probably present their arguments more cogently than the conscientious but diffident teacher at the infant level. There is a danger, therefore, that the opinions and suggestions of the latter sector of the education system may receive neither the respect nor the attention in educational and public spheres which they deserve.

The school and teacher variables appeared to have only a very limited effect; indeed, differences in relation to the teacher's social class origin were noticeably absent. There were some minor differences between teachers in the different social areas; for instance, teachers in lower working-class areas appreciated the comparatively greater freedom to experiment and innovate, although there was some suggestion that these same teachers were more likely to tend to denigrate the channels of mass culture associated with the areas in which they worked—films and television. Once again, there were few differences in relation to school organization, and they were not such as to differentiate clearly two types of teachers. Differences regarding teachers' position in the school were closely related to differences in status and role-set of class teachers and heads in the structure of the infant school. For example, heads found contacts with parents more satisfying than the class teachers did, possibly because (a) their position provided them with authority which was a compensation for their infant school status, (b) the tasks they had to carry out and the demands made on their organizing ability provided them with more intellectual stimulus, and (c) they had more opportunities for putting their ideals into practice.

Findings: (b) Teachers' attitudes to pupils' home background

An attitude scale was devised with sub-scales in the areas of relationships with parents, children, and the effectiveness of the school. It was found that a teacher's attitude to pupils' home background was very significantly associated with the personality dimension of authoritarianism. Generally, the more democratic teachers tended to have more favourable attitudes towards their pupils' home background.

Teachers' attitudes to this factor were not significantly related to the school social area[1] or organization, or to the teacher's social-class origin. However, in regard to one of the areas of expression of the attitude—relationships with children—heads had more favourable attitudes than class teachers (5% level of significance), and female heads had more favourable attitudes than male heads (5%).

Although total attitude scores were highly associated with authoritarianism, in relation to the three areas of expression of the attitude, authoritarianism was most closely associated with relationships with parents (1%), and least with relationships with children (not significant).

The sub-scale scores and total attitude score were examined in relation to a number of variables which previous research indicated might be influential other than the four school and teacher ones. It was found that a teacher's attitude to pupils' home background

---

[1] Bacchus reported in his study (1967) that social area mattered a great deal; teachers working in schools in the 'middle-class' areas tended to give a more favourable picture of the secondary modern pupil than those in the more 'working-class' areas (difference significant to the 3% level). However, it should be noted that in Bacchus' study the measure of social class was a composite, subjective one made by the heads, the research worker and the local educational officer, and this may have been affected by teachers' professional inferences about social areas, whereas the assessment in the present study was an objective one based on Census data. It is of interest in the present study that neither total attitude score nor even the sub-scale score on effectiveness of the school were significantly related to social area. There was a significant association between attitude to the effectiveness of the school and authoritarianism, the more authoritarian teacher tending to be pessimistic about the school's ability to influence pupils' values (5%). In the research on the authoritarian personality (Adorno, *et al.*, 1950) the rigid adherence to conventional middle-class values or 'conventionalism' has been described as characteristic of this personality type. Therefore, one would expect to find that the authoritarian teacher has a greater psychological need to conform to outside values, such as the inferences which teachers as a professional group tend to make about the different social areas.

was not significantly related to the teacher's age,[1] political philosophy, level of anxiety, marital status, place of birth, or teaching preferences, as to the type of child taught or type of planning.   Although only at a low level of statistical significance (5%) two relationships may be of educational importance.   Firstly, *heads*, dissatisfied with the status accorded to the teacher's position by the community, had a significantly lower mean score on the sub-scale attitude to the effectiveness of the school.   In other words, it was those heads who were anxious about their own status in the local community who were most likely to be pessimistic about the school's ability to influence pupils' values.   Secondly, the sub-scale dealing with relationships with parents and the total attitude score correlated significantly with the type of instruction the teacher preferred. Teachers who liked *group* instruction best were more likely to have unfavourable attitudes to pupils' parents and to pupils' home backgrounds generally.   The type of instruction preferred, group or individual, was not significantly related to any of the other variables considered, not even—as perhaps might have been expected—to authoritarianism.

Findings: (c) *The head's personality and attitudes and pupils' reading attainment*

Procedure.   An attempt was made to examine the level of *school* reading attainment in relation to the factors of the head's personality and attitudes, controlling the variable of school social area but not that of organization.   Controlling school social area produced small numbers in each of the three groupings; further, two of the measures used for reading attainment—estimated reading attainment and reading progress—used small range scales—six points for the former, and three points for the latter.   Thus, it was not expected that many significant relationships would be found.   Nevertheless, it was felt that an attempt to establish significant correlations might reveal trends worth further exploration, and provide guidance in making plans for future research.

School reading attainment was measured in relation to four aspects: tested reading attainment (mean score on a group test of

[1] Bacchus reported that the youngest and oldest teachers in his study held more unfavourable views about their pupils.   In the present study with infant teachers, the relationship between teacher's age and attitude to pupils' home background was not significantly related, although the association between teacher's age and the personality dimension of authoritarianism reached a low level of significance (5% level of significance), older teachers tending to be more authoritarian.

reading comprehension), estimated reading attainment (the mean book level), reading progress (class teachers' mean estimate of pupils' progress) and reading prediction (class teachers' estimate of prediction of final level of attainment). The test scores and estimated book levels for 1961 (the second year of infant schooling), the progress estimate made at the end of the summer term 1961, and the prediction completed half way through the autumn term were the four reading measures used in the analysis.

It was expected in the light of the other findings of this research that within the social area groupings of schools, the head's personality and attitudes would be most likely to affect school standards —for instance, teachers' estimates of pupils' progress and predictions of success—although, as previous research has indicated (Delaney, 1954; Davidson and Lang, 1960), it was quite possible that the actual level of pupils' reading attainment might be affected by the teacher's levels of expectation.

Head's personality. Table F/IX, in Appendix F (p. 164), shows the correlations for authoritarianism and the four measures of pupils' reading attainment. The relationship was examined over the whole sample of schools, and within each of the three social area groupings, so that the school social area variable was held constant. Only one relationship was significant: among schools in the upper working-class areas, heads with more authoritarian views tended to be associated with favourable estimates of pupils' progress by their class teachers.

Within social areas, there was no significant association between the head's personality and the school's estimated and tested level of reading attainment.

One might expect pupils' attitudes towards the academic values to be more positive amongst schools in the higher social areas and, therefore, that in these schools the head's personality would tend to be less effective. In the higher social area, the role of the head is probably much more clearly defined by the attitudes and expectations of pupils, parents and teachers. In the lower working-class areas, the expression of authoritarian attitudes by the head is likely to be in keeping with parents' expectations, and the latter tend to prepare their children for a passive role as pupils. However, the teachers' implication that middle-class values are superior, and particularly their stressing of the importance of academic interests, may provoke resentment or hostility in the pupils as they continue through the school system. In the higher social areas, pupils are, by reason of their background and parents' attitudes, likely to work to obtain academic goals irrespective of the head's personality; whereas, in the lower working-class areas, pupils are much more likely to be affected by the general atmosphere of the school and its level of morale, which are usually directly influenced by the head's personality and attitudes.

This study does not provide evidence of a significant association between pupils' attainment and head's personality in the lowest social area, where one would expect such an association to be most clearly apparent. Apart from the statistical limitations already considered, there may be several explanations as to why this did not occur. Firstly, one would expect such a relationship to be most apparent in regard to tested attainment, since this was the most objective of the three achievement assessments (tested, estimated attainment, estimated progress); but we have no information about the relationship between head's personality, school atmosphere and particular learning situations. For instance, the type of school atmosphere encouraged by the authoritarian head may be such as to facilitate group testing conditions. The results in relation to tested attainment might have been different if the pupils in all the lower working-class areas had been equally familiar with group test conditions. Probably a more fundamental difficulty was the inability, in this study, to control school organization *within* social area. No information is available about the effect of school organization on a head's personal influence, and certainly it is not easy to predict exactly how this would operate. Although the combined department schools tend to be smaller, the infant department may function under the control of a woman deputy or the top-infant class teacher, rather than the head who, if a male teacher, may be unfamiliar with infant teaching methods and less at ease with younger pupils. In these conditions, the influence of the head's personality may be lessened. Similarly, although the infant only schools tend to be larger, it does not follow automatically that the head of this type of school is less influential than the head of a combined department.

Head's attitude to pupils' home background. Table F/X, in Appendix F (p. 164), shows the correlations between the head's attitude to this factor and the four reading attainment variables. With school area controlled, in lower working-class schools the association between the head's attitudes and the school level of tested attainment and the class teachers' predictions fell just short of the 5% level of significance. Heads with favourable attitudes to pupils tended, in the lower working-class areas, to be associated with better tested reading attainment and more optimistic predictions from the class teachers.

Over the total group of schools, the nearest miss was in relation to the head's attitudes and the predictions of the teachers in their school. This association was just short of the 5% level; heads with favourable attitudes to pupils being associated with class teachers' favourable predictions.[1]

[1] Perhaps at this point a study by Johnson (1966) on teachers' attitudes to educational research might be mentioned as relevant. She considered that one of the most interesting of her findings was that attitudes towards research were shown to vary from school to school, and to reflect the favourable or unfavourable attitude shown by the head teacher. She suggested that, although the explanation of this fact was somewhat complex, the finding did support the increasing tendency to regard research into the head's role as crucial.

References

ADORNO, T. W., *et al.* (1950). *The Authoritarian Personality.* New York: Harper; ch. XIV.

BACCHUS, M. K. (1967). 'Some factors influencing the views of secondary modern school teachers on their pupils' interests and abilities', *Educ. Res.*, 9, 2, 147-50.

BIRCH, L. B. (1963). 'The teacher as learner'. *Bull. of the Brit. Psych. Soc.*, XVI, no. 50, 12-7.

DAVIDSON, H. H. and LANG, G. (1960). 'Children's perceptions of their teachers' feelings toward them related to self perception, school achievement and behaviour', *J. Exp. Educ. Psychol.*, 29, 2, 107-18.

DELANEY, M. (1954). 'An investigation into children's dependence on and reactions to a teacher's judgement with regard to their success or failure in school work'. M.A. thesis, University of London.

DEPARTMENT OF EDUCATION AND SCIENCE: CENTRAL ADVISORY COUNCIL FOR EDUCATION (ENGLAND). (1967). 'The 1964 National Survey: Data from the schools', Appendix 5. *Children and their Primary Schools.* (Plowden Report) London: H.M. Stationery Office.

HALL, J. and CARADOG-JONES, D. (1950). 'The social grading of occupations', *Brit. J. Sociol.*, I, 1.

JOHNSON, M. E. B. (1966). 'Teachers' attitudes to educational research', *Educ. Res.*, 9, 1, 74-9.

MAYS, J. B. (1962). *Education and the Urban Child.* Liverpool: Liverpool University Press.

RUDD, W. G. A. and WISEMAN, S. (1962). Sources of dissatisfaction among a group of teachers', *Brit. J. Educ. Psychol.*, XXXVII, 1, 10-21.

CHAPTER VII

A Note on Future Research

GENERALLY a head's personality did not appear to be significantly related to his school's standards, teachers' records of progress, or pupils' reading attainment. However, the heads' attitudes to pupils' home backgrounds were important in relation to their staffs' expectations of pupils' level of achievement by the end of the infant course—favourable attitudes on the part of the head being associated with optimistic predictions by the class teachers. It seems likely that the expression of a head's attitudes, involving inferences and judgements about the abilities of pupils, was able to influence his staff's expectations of pupils.

This factor of heads' attitudes to pupils' home backgrounds may be of more importance in particular social areas, but very little definite evidence was obtained from this study on this point. The numbers of schools involved in each social area were too small to give much precision to the measurements. It would certainly be worth investigating in future research the relationship between the general atmosphere of the school (the teachers' level of expectation) and pupils' tested reading attainment. We know from previous research that teacher's approval can not only maintain but actually raise pupils' estimates of their own abilities. It is therefore feasible that amongst lower working-class pupils, favourable teacher attitudes may create the sort of school atmosphere in which these types of pupils are able to achieve a higher level of reading attainment than either they or their teachers may have believed possible. What one would like to see is an experiment carried out in a larger group of these schools, with the factor of school organization controlled.

In middle-class area schools, pupils' attitudes are more consistently orientated towards valuing education. They are less likely to be affected by the attitudes of their teachers, although the latter's expectations may be an important factor. Teachers in these areas tend to believe that their pupils are more highly motivated to learn to read, but parental interest may mean pressure on the school for pupils to achieve particular standards, especially in relation to pupils' progress. There is evidence from the present study that the middle- and upper working-class area teachers were dissatisfied with their opportunities for freedom of action in the classroom. It seems likely, therefore, that teachers in middle-class areas are more controlled by the expectations of the community they serve, and by the formal, well-established conventions of the school system than are their colleagues in the working-class areas. As a result of these social pressures, and because of their own professional expectations and inferences, they may tend to over-estimate pupils' abilities and attainments. It is quite possible that it was this uneasy, over-stressing of academic success, combined with the teacher's more formal and impersonal role, which acted as an inhibiting influence on the attainment of these pupils and possibly helps to explain why they were not so markedly superior to the upper working-class pupils as might have been expected.

Undoubtedly the values of the community which the school serves are important as an influence on the actual rather than the formal functioning of the school as a social system. The school in its institutional function, with roles for pupil and teacher, will operate in various ways in different social conditions and permit various permutations on teacher-pupils relationships; and these in turn will affect the level of pupil attainment. A continuation of the study of the sociology of the primary school is needed not only to provide further information about the effectiveness of the head's role in different social areas, but also to provide evidence as to how different-ly organized infant schools function and succeed in different social environments. Studies along these lines might enable some evalua-tion to be made of the importance of the factor of the teacher's sex in regard to the development of a school's philosophy and values, and might also throw some light on the complex question of teachers' assessments of pupils of different sex.

Yet another topic which would seem to require further exploration is that of the relationship between the teacher's personality and choice of method of teaching reading. In the present study, the numbers were too small to produce any conclusive evidence regarding choice of method and teacher satisfaction, but a study which examin-ed the relationship between these factors with the variables of school organization and social area controlled would be valuable. In the light of the findings of this present study, it would seem possible that the phonic and look-and-say or sentence methods of teaching reading, may possibly appeal to teachers of markedly diverse personalities.

74

Appendices

A. SELECTION OF SCHOOLS

B. QUESTIONNAIRES AND FORMS

C. ADDITIONAL INFORMATION, CHAPTER II

D. ADDITIONAL INFORMATION, CHAPTER IV

E. ADDITIONAL INFORMATION, CHAPTER V

F. ADDITIONAL INFORMATION, CHAPTER VI

G. BIBLIOGRAPHY

Selection of Schools

Method

IN 1958 there were 607 Primary Schools in the London County Council Education Authority. One in six of these schools were sampled, the method being to number alphabetically the schools within each type of school organization and educational division, and then, using a table of random numbers, to select an appropriate number of schools from each group. In this way 100 schools were selected, the sample being representative of London schools generally in relation to school type and educational division. A further 20 schools were selected in the same way, to be used as a replacement sample if selected schools were unable to take part. All 120 schools were sent the initial questionnaire; 71 returned completed questionnaires (59 per cent return).

It was considered that a larger group than 71 might be required at certain stages of the analysis of data, and for this reason a further 61 schools were chosen, again at random, from the whole population, with stratification of organization and division. The additional 61 schools were arranged in random order for replacement purposes, in the same way as the original replacement sample of 20. Of these further 61 schools, 29 returned completed questionnaires (48 per cent return).

Thus 181 schools were approached, 100 of which co-operated in the survey stage of the research. Fourteen of the schools completing *Initial Questionnaires* were not willing to take part in the two-year investigation. Of the 86 schools which began the two-year project, 13 did not continue after the first year, and eight did not complete the second year.

The proportion of non-respondents tended to lessen at each stage of the research, probably because once personal relationships had been established between the schools and the investigators, it was easier to keep in touch with schools and explain the value of their co-operation and individual contribution to the research.

Non-respondents' reasons for refusing to take part in the research

It was possible to examine the replies of the non-respondents and to analyse their reasons for non-co-operation. Of the original one-in-six sample, 45 per cent were non-respondents and of these, three-quarters gave reasons. Most commonly mentioned reasons were:

(1) staffing difficulties or shortage of staff

(2) difficulties in staffing the reception class

(3) taking part in another inquiry

(4) head newly appointed or about to retire

(5) size of school

(6) school newly opened

There were 21 schools which did not reply to the original letter asking for their assistance, or to the follow-up letter. These schools did not differ significantly from the co-operating schools in relation to type of organization or educational division.

Eight of the 14 schools which refused to take part in the two-year project gave similar reasons to those cited above; the other six did not give reasons. Of the 21 schools which withdrew during the next two years, 15 gave as reasons: (1) staffing difficulties; (2) size of school; and (3) pressure of work. Seven schools did not continue with the project because the head fell ill or a new head was appointed.

Comparison of groups of schools at each stage of the research

The selected schools at each stage of the research were representative of London Primary Schools as a whole with respect to organization, religious denomination and social area. From the survey stage onwards there was a greater degree of co-operation from one particular educational Division, whilst two Divisions tended to be under-represented. This trend did not, however, affect the representative nature of the research schools in relation to the three factors of school organization, religious denomination and social area.

Questionnaires and Forms

1. *Initial Questionnaire.* (Head and reception class teacher's forms, April 1959).

2. *Home Background* (*General*) *Form.* (Autumn term 1960).

3. *Home Background* (*Individual*) *Form.* (Spring term 1961).

4. *Personal Questionnaire.* (Autumn-Spring terms 1960-61).

5. *Reading Readiness Estimate.* (Autumn terms 1959-60).

6. *Primer Criterion.* (Summer terms 1960-61).

---

1. *Initial Questionnaire* (designed by J. M. Morris and E. J. Goodacre).

The questionnaire was designed in three sections; the first and second (by J. M. Morris) referred to matters of practice and reading materials, the third (by E. J. Goodacre) dealt with teachers' means of assessing the social background of pupils and details of material environment of the school. Questionnaires were completed by 198 heads and reception class teachers in 100 schools during May 1959.

Teachers and their Pupils' Home Background

INITIAL QUESTIONNAIRE HEAD TEACHER'S FORM

| Head Teacher

NATIONAL FOUNDATION FOR EDUCATIONAL RESEARCH

Primary School Studies—Teaching Beginners to Read

Name of Head Teacher..

Name of School...........................Education Division................

Type of Organization (e.g. Junior Mixed and Infants, Infants only,
etc.)

....

Number of infants on roll at end of the Christmas

Term 1958...

Number of reception class teachers...

Address of School...

Telephone No..

---

*Where there is a box answer,
would you please tick the appropriate box/boxes.*

SECTION A

1. Which of the following reading methods are used in your infant
    school/department?

alphabetic	phonic	look and say	sentence

Head Teacher

2. (a) Does the main approach to the teaching of reading in your infant school/department tend to be

Informal	
Formal	

(b) How would you describe this approach to an interested parent?

3. What would you say are the main considerations which dictate the type of instruction given in your infant school/department?

4. Is the children's interest in reading aroused in any particular way in your infant school/department?

5. In the teaching of reading in your infant school/department does a change of emphasis take place at any stage?

Yes	

No	

Please elaborate your answer

....

6. Would you please indicate the number of teachers in the infant school/department?

(a)

Men	
Women	

D

Head Teacher

(b)

Under 25 yrs.		25-40 yrs.		40+ yrs.	
married	single	married	single	married	single

(c) Number of teachers who were trained for teaching infants in their college course? ....

(d) Number of teachers who have had more than one year's experience in an infant school/department? ....

SECTION B

1. (a) Is a basic scheme used throughout the infant school/department, e.g. 'Happy Venture', 'Janet and John', 'Beacon', etc.? Please name the scheme or series used.

   (b) Would you please say why this particular scheme or series is used?

   (c) If a basic scheme is used, is it supplemented by readers from other schemes or series? Please name them and say why they are used.

   (d) Would you please estimate the percentage of pupils who, at the end of their infant course, are able to read (as judged by their progress in the basic reading scheme).

Book 4 or beyond	
Books 2 or 3	
Book 1 and below	
	100%

Appendix B

2. Are children allowed to take
    their basic readers home?

Yes	
No	

3. (a) Do the teachers in your infant school/
         department use reading apparatus?

Yes	
No	

    (b) Is this apparatus

         published with the readers [ ]

         made by the teachers? [ ]

    (c) Is this apparatus used
         for class purposes:
         e.g. wall charts,
         flash cards, etc.
         for individual
         purposes, e.g.
         matching, etc.?

Published apparatus	Teacher made

4. (a) Is there an infant school/department
         library?

Yes	

No	

83

Head Teacher

(b)   Is there a special room to house it?

| Yes | |

| No | |

(c)   How is it organized?...

(d)   Are children allowed to take library books home?

| Yes | |

| No | |

| all | |

(e)   Do | some | | teachers have their own library corners in their class rooms?

| no | |

(f)   What are your sources for obtaining books for either the library or library corners?

5.   (a)   Are any tests used in your infant school/department? Please name them.

(b)   Would you please say why you use these tests?

6.   (a)   Do you think the term 'backward' in reading can be applied to children in the infant school?

(b)   What provision, if any, is made for 'backward' readers in your infant school/department?

7.   What do you understand by the term 'reading readiness'?

Appendix B

SECTION C

1. (a) Would you please tick the appropriate space in column **A**
if your infant school/department has the following:

		A	B
i	A staffroom i		
ii	A hall not used as a canteen or classroom ii		
	A hall used as canteen not class-room		
	A hall not used as canteen but as a classroom		
iii	Large rooms with good windows iii		
iv	Modern chairs and tables in class-rooms iv		
v	Sinks in classrooms v		
vi	Separate stockroom and plenty of cupboards vi		
	No stockroom but cupboards ..		
vii	Electric lighting vii		
viii	Good sanitation and hot water .. viii		
	Good sanitation but no hot water		
	Bad sanitation but hot water ..		
ix	Cloakroom as a special room with pegs and lockers for each child ix		
x	Playground for infants use only .. x		
xi	Good location (e.g. open site, quiet, etc.) xi		
xii	Attractive general appearance .. xii		

(b) Please give the approximate date when the infant school/
department building was erected...

(c) Has this building been enlarged or altered in any way since
this date? ....

Head Teacher

2. (a) What part do you think a child's home background plays in learning to read? Please elaborate.

3. Would you please indicate by a tick in the appropriate column, in how many of your pupils' families

	Many	Some	Few	Don't know
(a) the mother goes out to work				
(b) the family has its own telephone				
(c) holidays are taken outside the British Isles				
(d) the family has sole use of a garden				

4. *Without questioning the children*, would you please estimate the approximate percentage of your pupils

(a)

who are only children	
who come from a family of 2 children	
,, ,, ,, ,, ,, ,, 3 ,,	
,, ,, ,, ,, ,, ,, 4 ,,	
	100%

86

Head Teacher

(b)   whose parents are in the age group

under 25 yrs.	
25-40	
40+	
	100%

5. *Without questioning the children,* would you please indicate the approximate percentage of your present pupils who fall into the following rough classifications of fathers' occupations:

Occupation	%
Professional workers..	
Clerical workers	
Skilled workers	
Semi-skilled workers..	
Unskilled workers	
	100%

6. Have you a parent-teachers' association in the school? If so, would you please describe it briefly.

Yes	

No	

87

	Head Teacher

7. (a) Do you have

a lot of	

some	

absenteeism?

not much	

Would you please give, in order of importance, the types of reasons the children usually have for being absent

....

....

(b) Would you please estimate the approximate percentage of attendance per year?

.... %

(c)

a lot of	

some	

lateness in the mornings?

not much	

Would you please give in order of importance the types of reasons the children usually have for being late...........................

....

8. (a) Do you at any time visit the homes of your pupils? If so, in what circumstances?..

Yes			No	

Head Teacher

(b) Would you please estimate the approximate percentage of

parents who come to see you?..%

Would you please say in what circumstances.............................

9. (a) Are there any ways in which you are able to judge the level
of prosperity of the homes from which your pupils come?

Yes			No	

Please specify...

(b) Do you have any children from 'needy' families, and if so,
does the school make any provisions for them?

10. In what ways do parents show their desire for their children
to make progress in learning to read?

11. If you have any additional comments, perhaps you would like

to add them here..

Would you be willing to co-operate in a further investigation of
the problems raised in this questionnaire?

Yes	No

D*

INITIAL QUESTIONNAIRE RECEPTION CLASS TEACHER'S FORM

> Reception Class
> Teacher

NATIONAL FOUNDATION FOR EDUCATIONAL RESEARCH

Primary School Studies—Teaching Beginners to Read

Name of Reception Class Teacher...

Name of School...

Size of Class (at the beginning and end of Christmas Term 1958)

....beginning

....end

> *Where there is a box answer, would you please tick the appropriate box*

SECTION A

1. (a) Would you please say how many of the children in your class come from a nursery school/class?

   (b) Have you noticed any differences between these children and those who have had no nursery experience?

2. Would you please estimate the percentage of your pupils, who had already begun to read from a book when they first came to school (i.e. September, 1958)?

   .... %

3. How do you recognize readiness to read in your pupils?

> Reception Class
> Teacher

4. (a) Which methods do you use in commencing to teach reading?

all	

(b) Is systematic phonic | some | | pupils?
instruction given to

no	

(c) Please elaborate your answer..

5. Do you use any tests? Please name them.

6. Do you aim at any specific standard before sending your children to the next class? (Please specify the standard)

7. (a) Do you systematically follow a published reading scheme/ series? Please name it.

(b) If you use a scheme/series, are any children allowed to take the basic readers home? (Please give your reasons)

SECTION B

1. Were you trained in infant method in your college course?

....

2. How long have you taught in infant or nursery schools?

....years

3. Have you had any nursery experience? Please give details.

> Reception Class
> Teacher

SECTION C

1. (a) What part do you think a child's home background plays in the initial stages of learning to read? Please elaborate.

   (b) What would you say are the characteristics of a *good* home background?

   (c) What would you say are the characteristics of a *poor* home background?

2. Would you please estimate the approximate percentage of children in your class, who usually come to school

with a parent	
with a brother or sister	
with other children	
with a maid or mother's help ..	
with a neighbour or other mother..	
by themselves..	
	100%

3. (a) Do you have

a lot of	
some	
not much	

absenteeism?

Would you please give in order of importance, the types of reasons the children usually have for being absent.................

Appendix B

(b) Would you please estimate the approximate percentage of attendance per year?

.... %

(c) Do you have

a lot of	

some	

lateness in the mornings?

not much	

Would you please give in order of importance the types of reasons the children usually have for being late

4. (a) Do you at any time visit the homes of your pupils?

....

In what circumstances?..

(b) Would you please estimate the approximate percentage of parents who come to see you?.. %

In what circumstances? ....

5. Are there any ways in which you are able to judge the level of prosperity of the homes from which your pupils come?

Yes	

No	

Please specify..

6. In what ways do the parents of your pupils show their desire for their children to make progress in learning to read?

If you have any additional comments, perhaps you would like to add them here..

93

2. *Home Background* (*General*) *Form* (E. J. Goodacre)

The teachers were asked in this form to rate on a qualitative scale items suggested by those teachers completing the *Initial Questionnaire* as characteristics of the 'good' home. The form also requested further information regarding the teacher's ability to assess the school's social status, using the criterion of pupil's parental occupation, their estimates in general terms of their pupils' parental interest, intellectual ability and quality of home background, and for their opinion regarding the ability to learn to read of children from 'poor' homes.

Forms were completed by 275 heads and class teachers during the Autumn term, 1960. Of the 100 schools who completed *Initial Questionnaires* in May 1959, 86 consented to take part in the two-year follow-up investigation, starting in September 1959. During the first year, 13 schools withdrew for various reasons. Of the 73 who began the second year, 64 schools completed the *Home Background* (*General*) *Form*. The staffs of two schools objected strongly to being asked to complete this form and did not do so, although consenting to remain in the research. Three schools objected and left the research giving as their reason, their staff's reaction to the form. One school agreed to complete the form but refused to co-operate in completing the *Home Background* (*Individual*) *Form* requesting information about individual children's home conditions.

CHILDREN'S HOME BACKGROUND (GENERAL) FORM

SCHOOL CODE..

Please indicate with a tick in the appropriate column how you feel about the following aspects of children's home background. Please be certain to answer each item.

			I FEEL IT IS				
			Most Im-portant	Im-portant	Un-decided	Less Im-portant	Un-portant
C.	1. that parents are interested in their children's activities	1.					
	2. that parents are prepared to spend time with their children playing, talking or reading to them ..	2.					
	3. that parents answer and explain their children's questions	3.					
	4. that parents can stimulate and help their children to carry out ideas, etc. ..	4.					
	5. that the parents are intelligent, educated people ..	5.					
A.	6. that parents help the child with his school work ..	6.					
	7. that parents show an interest in the child's school progress	7.					
	8. that parents are interested in education for its own sake	8.					
F.	9. that there is good conversation and correct speech in the home	9.					
	10. that there are good manners and social habits	10.					
	11. that the home is culturally rich, with the right amusements, sensible toys, etc. ..	11.					
	12. that there is travel and holidays	12.					
	13. visits to interesting places and events	13.					
	14. familiarity with books and appreciation of reading ..	14.					

95

	I FEEL IT IS				
	Most Im-portant	*Im-portant*	*Un-decided*	*Less Im-portant*	*Im-portant*
E. 15. firm but kindly discipline 15.					
16. a sense of moral and spiritual values.. 16.					
17. a religious faith .. .. 17.					
D. 18. that meals, sleep, habits are regular 18.					
19. that television watching is planned 19.					
20. that there is cleanliness .. 20.					
B. 21. that the family is united and they are mutually considerate 21.					
22. that the child is loved and wanted for his own sake.. 22.					
23. that the home life is stable 23.					
G. 24. that the home is not overcrowded 24.					
25. that there is space to play 25.					
26. that the family is financially secure 26.					
27. that the parents enjoy good health 27.					
28. that the mother is not working 28.					
29. that if the mother is working, she makes provision for the children after school hours 29.					

| | | I FEEL IT IS | | | |
	Most Im- portant	Im- portant	Un- decided	Less Im- portant	Un- portant
H. 30. that there is good, sensible food .. .. .. 30.					
31. that there is good, sensible clothing .. .. .. 31.					
32. that the children are ade- quately clothed and fed .. 32.					
33. that the children are sent to bed early .. .. .. 33.					
34. that the children have adequate sleep .. .. 34.					
35. that the parents were born in this country .. .. 35.					
36. that there is a good home background .. .. 36.					

1. Would you please estimate approximately (by putting a tick in the appropriate space) how many of your pupils' parents come into the following rough groupings of parental occupations.

OCCUPATION	ALL	MOST	SOME	FEW	NONE
Professional					
Clerical					
Skilled					
Semi-skilled					
Unskilled					

97

2. Would you please give examples in each column of the type of occupation you associate with each of these groups of occupations.

OCCUPATIONS	EXAMPLES	
Professional	1.	2.
Clerical	1.	2.
Skilled	1.	2.
Semi-skilled	1.	2.
Unskilled	1.	2.

3. Here are nine types of occupation. Would you please rank them from 1 to 9 in order of social standing, placing the number 1 against the number of the occupation you consider has the most social standing and the number 9 against that with the least.

RANK	OCCUPATION
	Auctioneer
	Gas Fitter
	Infant Teacher
	Cashier
	Commercial Traveller
	Headmaster (Primary school)
	Docker
	Garage Hand
	Doctor

Would you please put a tick under the one word of the five given words (all, most, some, few, none), which you feel best expresses your opinion on the particular subject. We have left several lines under each question, where you might like to add any qualification you feel may be necessary.

4. Would you say that

all	most	some	few	none

of the parents of your pupils are interested in their children's progress? (Please put a tick under the word which you think is most appropriate.)

....

5. Would you say that

all	most	some	few	none

of these children are of above average intellectual ability?

....

6. Would you say that

all	most	some	few	none

of these children have good home backgrounds?

....

7. Do you think that

all	most	some	few	none

of the children who come from a poor home background can learn to read?

....

99

8. Perhaps you would like to add here any comments that you may
    have about the questions that we have asked, or any points
    that you think might be of interest to us in connection with the
    subject of teaching children and their home background.

    ....

    ....

                        Signed..(Head, class teacher)

    ————————————

3. *Home Background* (*Individual*) *Form* (E. J. Goodacre).

This form requested information from the teachers on pupils'
home conditions, personality characteristics, and attributes on the
basis of individual children. Its purpose was, firstly, to discover
whether teachers differed in their estimates when asked to assess the
background of individual children instead of pupils in general;
secondly, to secure evidence of teachers' attitudes to their pupils'
background—a teacher's ability to record information about
individual pupils' home conditions was accepted as evidence of an
interest in and, therefore, an attitude towards pupils' home background; thirdly, to relate individual children's reading attainment
and progress to factors which might be relevant to reading success
or failure.

Forms were completed by 163 teachers in 64 schools during the
Spring Term, 1961 on 3,250 individual pupils—the 1954 age group
in their second year of infant schooling. The number of teachers
completing these forms was smaller than that for the completion of
Home Background (*General*) *Forms* because only class teachers of
the 1954 age-group pupils were asked for their estimates, whereas
all infant teachers were asked to complete the *Home Background*
(*General*) *Forms*.

Appendix B

HOME BACKGROUND (INDIVIDUAL) FORM

SCHOOL CODE................................

CHILD'S NAME

Child's *Class*   ..   ..

Home Background
CODE................   No=1.   Yes=2.
Don't know=0.   Confidential=4.

1. Do the parents help this child with school work?   1.

2. Is this child familiar with and appreciative of books?   2.

3. Does this child come from a home where there is a well ordered routine, e.g. meals, sleep, habits?   3.

4. Does this child come from an emotionally stable home?   4.

5. Does this child come from a home where the mother does not go out to work, or if she does, she makes provision for the child after school hours?   5.

6. Does this child seem to get enough sleep?   6.

7. Does this child come from a home where housing conditions are satisfactory?   7.

8. Do the parents show an interest in this child's school progress?   8.

9. Is this child's television watching planned, supervised?   9.

10. Do the parents take an interest in this child's activities? (e.g. child's questions, interests, ideas)   10.

SCHOOL CODE..

CHILD'S NAME

Child's *Class* .. ..

Personality
CODE................... No=1. Yes=2. Unable to
say=0. Child rarely seen, e.g. sickness,
school absence=3

Is this child (1) Happy? 1.

(2) Active? 2.

(3) Generous? 3.

(4) Naughty? 4.

(5) Polite? 5.

(6) Dirty? 6.

(7) Undersized? 7.

(8) Talkative? 8.

(9) Untidy? 9.

(10) Apathetic? 10.

(11) Humourous? 11.

(12) Enterprising? 12.

(13) Lazy? 13.

(14) Healthy? 17.

N.B. It is stressed that on behalf of the Foundation, we do not wish you to ask the children themselves or their parents questions about their home background.

SCHOOL CODE..

CHILD'S NAME

Child's *Class* ..   ..

Additional Items
CODE...................... Put the number in the brackets of the answer which you think is most appropriate to this child.
It is the number in front which applies.

. Child is (1) frequently absent; (2) sometimes; (3) rarely absent   1.

. Child (1) likes school very much; (2) likes school on the whole more than he dislikes it; (3) resents school   2.

. Child comes from (1) good; (2) poor home background. Don't know=0   3.

. Child is of (1) above average intellectual ability; (2) average; (3) below average intellectual ability   4.

. Child (1) does better in reading than one would expect; (2) does much as one would expect; (3) does less well than one would expect   5.

SCHOOL CODE..

CHILD'S NAME

Child's *Class*   ..   ..

6. Would you please rate the interest which parents show in their child's school progress and the encouragement they give according to the following 3-point scale: (1) very interested in child's education; visit school frequently for the purpose of inquiring into progress made; offer every encouragement to child. (2) Moderately interested, but offer only average encouragement; sometimes visit school. (3) Show no interest in child's progress and give no encouragement; never, or hardly ever, seen at school   6.

Additional Facts about these particular children.

....

N.B.   Have you remembered to enter the class under each child's name?   Thank you.

Signed (1)... Teacher of Class................

(2)... Teacher of Class................

(3)... Teacher of Class................

(4)... Teacher of Class................

N.B.   It is stressed that on behalf of the Foundation, we do not wish you to ask the children themselves or their parents questions about their home background.

Appendix B

School Code...

Spring Term

ESTIMATES OF INDIVIDUAL CHILDREN

Completion of the forms

In a number of studies of individual children who experience difficulty in learning to read, it has been found that emotional troubles, and difficulties in the home play an important part. For this reason, we considered it desirable to have a record from you of any difficulties which you feel may explain an individual child's lack of progress at school. In many cases you may not have the information required, or you may feel particular items on the forms are of little importance in general teaching. We hope the code we have provided for completing the forms will help you and cover all possibilities, but if you feel there is any additional fact we should know about, would you please be good enough to add this at the end in the appropriate space.

We fully realize the limitations imposed by categories in this type of form, and that this information can never provide us with the full and complete knowledge of individual children possessed by teachers. But we assure you that such form-filling is not a waste of time, since it can enable us to gain some idea of the problems with which you are coping and possible explanations of individual children's success or failure.

As you will see, we have asked you for information about the children under two main headings, 'Home Background' and 'Personality'. The items under the first heading are those things about the child's home life which you feel may give that child an advantage or disadvantage. If you should feel that any information is confidential to yourself alone, would you please use the appropriate code.

With regard to Personality, we have used adjectives most commonly used by teachers in talking to each other about children's personalities. Here we are thinking of those aspects of personality, which may cause a child to have difficulty in getting on with either his fellows or his teacher, or in reverse, those qualities which enable him to adjust readily to the social climate of the classroom.

We have added some other items, such as school attendance and liking for school which you may feel are relevant to children's school progress.

105

In the completion of other estimates, we have found it is best if you take each item, and assess each child on this particular point, rather than go through the list of items one by one for each child. If a child has left will you please put a line through his name, or if we have omitted a child's name would you please add it. We are interested in any child born in 1954.

We realize that estimates take some time to complete properly, so we should like to emphasize how important they are to our re-research. This information is invaluable, and it is only you, the teachers, who can provide it. Knowing how many tasks come the teacher's way in the course of the school day, we should like to say how grateful we are when you can find time to help us with this important research. We hope this study will finally provide information helpful to the class teacher in her daily task of teaching children to read.

N.B. It is stressed that on behalf of the Foundation, we do not wish you to ask the children themselves or their parents questions about their home background.

---

4. *Personal Questionnaire* (E. J. Goodacre)

This questionnaire asked the teachers for information about themselves: age, education, teaching experience, etc. Also, it provided the opportunity to ask the teachers to complete certain attitude and personality scales, e.g. indicating how they felt towards parents and children, how they viewed the role and influence of the school, and whether they tended to be authoritarian in their general outlook.

In view of the very personal nature of the major part of this data, it was decided that the help of the heads of the schools should be enlisted at arranged meetings, followed by personal interviews with the entire infant staff of each of a selected group of schools. The main project had by that time involved the staffs of the research schools in considerable additional work, and it was decided that only approximately half the research schools should be asked for their co-operation in completing the *Personal Questionnaires* which had only an indirect bearing upon the reading project. Therefore, only 34 schools and their staffs were approached. The group of schools selected were representative of the total group of research schools in regard to type of school organization and social area.

The willingness of heads and members of staff to complete and return a *Personal Questionnaire* varied from school to school. However, the average return was 75 per cent for heads (all schools) and 76 per cent class teachers (34 selected schools). The questionaires were completed by a total of 148 heads and class teachers during the Autumn and Spring terms, 1960-61. In two schools, heads expressed the wish that their staffs should not be approached.

PERSONAL QUESTIONNAIRE

Strictly Confidential

Code No...

Date ....

Mr.
Name...Mrs.　School Code No..............
Miss

Please underline whichever applies.

(1)　Aged under 25,　26-35,　36-45,　46-55,　over 55.

(2)　Married,　widowed,　divorced,　single.

(3)　Male,　female.

(4)　Head teacher,　class teacher.

Please complete
(5)　Place of birth................................... Town............................... Country.

(6) Parental Occupation (as below)

	Major Occupation	Trade or Industry	If employee, indicate grade, rank and no. of people supervised	If employer, no. of employees
Example 1	Teacher	Primary School	Assistant	
Example 2	Clerk	Printing Works	10. (Chief Clerk)	
Father				
Mother before marriage				
Mother after marriage				

(7) Education and Training.

Name and Type of School, e.g. Council School, Private	From	To	Certificates or Degrees
Elementary			
Secondary			
University			
Professional Course(s)			

    (a) Were you trained to teach infants?...

    (b) Number of years teaching service.........................years.

    (c) Number of years spent in an infant school/department ....years.

    (d) How long have you been in your present appointment? ....

(8) Do you live in the same borough as that in which the school is situated?....................................

Would you please tell us about the major considerations which prompted you to apply for a post in this area of London

....

(9) Do you read a daily paper(s) regularly?......................................

Would you please name it/them..

....

Do you read a Sunday paper(s) regularly?..................................

Would you please name it/them..

....

Do you take any journal(s) or magazine(s) regularly? Would you please name it/them..

....

(10) Please rank the following pastimes in order of their importance to you, placing the 1 against the most important and 9 against the least.

RANK	PASTIMES
	Listening to the radio
	Reading the newspaper
	Reading magazines/journals
	Reading books
	Watching sports
	Listening to music
	Watching films
	Watching television
	Going to the theatre

Please give the names of other leisure activities you enjoy. Please give them in their order of importance to you, placing the most important first..

....

(11) Here is a list of various aspects of teaching which are often mentioned by teachers when they are talking about the satisfactions and dissatisfactions of teaching as a form of employment.

Please put the letter S against those aspects which you consider give you satisfaction, placing the number 1 beside the one which you find the most satisfying.

Then put the letter D against each aspect which you find dissatisfying, again placing the number 1 against the one you think is the most dissatisfying.

Please leave blank those items to which you feel indifferent.

	the social or human value of the job
	the holidays
	the opportunity for intellectual growth
	the environment (general surroundings)
	one's colleagues
	the contact with parents
	the salary
	the responsibility for others
	the independence of action
	the hours of employment
	the opportunity for self expression
	the possibility of undertaking out of school voluntary or paid activities of a social service nature
	the day to day variety of the job
	the opportunity to work with children
	the position given to teachers by the community
	the opportunities for promotion or advancement
	the opportunity of putting personal ideals into practice

Would you please add any additional satisfaction, dissatisfaction which you have found teaching offers you.

satisfaction..

dissatisfaction ....

(12) Which of the following in each group do you consider as the strongest, weakest, trait in your make-up? In each group there are four traits, please put the letter S against the one in each group you feel is your strongest, and the letter W against the one in each group you feel is your weakest.

A accuracy ....   B good judgement ....
    ambition ....   sympathy ....
    cheerfulness ....   originality ....
    decisiveness ....   conscientiousness ....

C common sense ....   D initiative ....
    enthusiasm ....   adaptibility ....
    leadership ....   alertness ....
    refinement ....   foresight ....

E thorough ....   F industrious ....
    resourceful ....   systematic ....
    selfconfident ....   good hearted ....
    truthful ....   cultured ....

(13) Which of the following would you prefer to do? In each of the three groups tick on the line against the item to show your preference.

1. teach
   (a) a class of children of widely varying
       ability?   ..   ..
   (b) a class of bright children? ..   ..
   (c) a class of slow or retarded children?   ....
   (d) a class of children of average ability?   ....

2. Whenever possible to have
   (a) children learning in a single unified
       group?   ..   ..
   (b) children learning in several small
       groups?   ..   ..
   (c) children individually?   ..   ..

111

3. Prefer to
    (a) plan your school work from day to day in the light of what seems appropriate? .. ..
    (b) have no definite scheme of work? .. ..
    (c) follow a planned scheme of work? .. ..
    (d) follow a planned scheme of work modified to suit the particular class? ....

(14) Here are some questions regarding the way people behave, feel and act. After each item there is a 'Yes' and a 'No'. Try and decide whether *you* usually act, feel or think in this way, then put a circle round the 'Yes' or the 'No'. Work quickly and do not spend too much time over any item. We want your first reaction, not a long drawnout thought process! Be sure not to omit any items. There are no right or wrong answers, and this is not a test of intelligence or ability, but simply a measure of the way you behave.

1.	Are you often startled at a sudden noise?	Yes	No
2.	Do you find you are never depressed for very long?	Yes	No
3.	Do you ever get palpitations of the heart when excited or upset?	Yes	No
4.	Do you think it would have been better to have lived in another age?	Yes	No
5.	Do you feel success is very much a matter of luck?	Yes	No
6.	Do you often have to go back and make sure of things, like turning off the light?	Yes	No
7.	Can you concentrate easily?	Yes	No
8.	Do you find your surroundings, both human and material, influence your decisions	Yes	No
9.	Do you ever get the feeling that something dreadful is going to happen? ..	Yes	No
10.	Do you feel most things can be achieved if one is sufficiently determined? ..	Yes	No
11.	Do you consider that you are more optimistic than most people?	Yes	No

112

12.	Do you sometimes feel worried about nothing in particular?	Yes	No
13.	Do you feel the world is by and large a happy place?	Yes	No
14.	Can you relax easily when sitting or lying down?	Yes	No
15.	Were you nervous as a child	Yes	No
16.	Have you found that usually things turn out better than you expected?	Yes	No
17.	Do you often get a sinking feeling in the stomach?	Yes	No
18.	Do you look forward to the future with confidence?	Yes	No
19.	Do you feel most people cannot really be trusted?	Yes	No
20.	Do you usually sleep well? ..	Yes	No

(15) The following statements refer to opinions about a number of topics with which some people agree and others disagree. Please mark each statement in the left-hand margin according to your agreement or disagreement as follows:

      1. for 'strongly agree'   3. for 'disagree'
      2. for 'agree'   4. for 'strongly disagree'

.... 1. Most children try to do their work to the best of their ability.

.... 2. Only too often the home undoes the work of the school.

.... 3. One can never change human nature.

.... 4. Every person should have complete faith in some supernatural power whose decisions he obeys without question.

.... 5. Few children try to tax the patience of their teachers.

.... 6. Most parents make an effort to be friendly with their children.

.... 7. If parents disagree with the aims of the school, they should take their children elsewhere.

.... 8. All children are fundamentally likeable.

.... 9. The money spent on education during the last decade might have been more usefully spent on other social services, e.g. widows' pensions.

.... 10. The school should make no attempt to justify its aims.

.... 11. For one to do a good job one needs to know what precisely the person in charge wants to be done and exactly how he thinks it should be done.

.... 12. The school has more opportunities to educate children in the widest sense, than it has ever had before.

.... 13. Few parents realize that their own children aren't perfect.

.... 14. The school can do much to modify the values a child acquires from home.

.... 15. Parents should be allowed on school premises at most times of the day.

.... 16. Nature is much more important than nurture.

.... 17. The school should be the centre for the intellectual and social development of the community.

.... 18. Obedience and respect for authority are the most important virtues children should learn at school.

.... 19. Parents usually cannot see the teacher's side of the problem when something happens at school.

.... 20. All children, if taught under ideal conditions, would be able to do better.

.... 21. The school is powerless to change standards of taste.

.... 22. If a child is difficult, there is really no way of getting him to learn.

.... 23. Parents are usually considerate of teachers' feelings.

.... 24. The school's function is to teach the basic skills, it cannot influence the way in which such skills are to be used.

.... 25. There are no bad children; there are only bad, or unskilled teachers.

.... 26. Children would rather look up to a teacher than treat him as an equal.

.... 27. The most teachers can hope to do is to ensure that most children enjoy their school days and look back on them with pleasure.

.... 28. Parents usually try to meet teachers half way.

Appendix B

Would you please read the following statements through and then mark each statement in the *left-hand* margin according to your agreement or disagreement as follows: A=agree. D=disagree.

Then would you please read the statements with which you have agreed, and in the *right-hand* column beside each put a tick in the appropriate column, telling us whether you consider such a change has been (1) for the better; (2) no effect; (3) for the worse.

A/D	STATEMENT	FOR THE BETTER	NO EFFECT	FOR THE WORSE
	1. The modern family is smaller than that of two or three generations ago.			
	2. Material standards of living for the working class have risen.			
	3. Attitudes to sexual morality and particularly to marriage have changed.			
	4. General cultural levels have changed.			
	5. An increasing number of the functions, rights and duties of the family are being taken over by the State, the schools and other outside bodies.			
	6. Religious belief has declined.			
	7. People's attitudes to property have changed.			
	8. School discipline has become less strict.			
	9. The influence of the school has declined.			
	10. To-day people talk more and work less.			
	11. The standard of candidates for the teaching profession has changed.			
	12. Hire purchase is much more widely used to-day.			
	13. Parental methods of child training have altered.			
	14. More children are at school for longer.			

Thank you for your help in completing this questionnaire. We appreciate your willingness to help us in our investigation, and we assure you that this additional information is of great value in our research.

5. *Reading Readiness Estimate* (J. M. Morris)

The reception class teachers were asked in the *Initial Questionnaire* to describe the characteristics which they considered were signs of a child's readiness to read. Although it was found that teachers depended primarily on attitudinal factors (child's interest and desire to learn to read) to recognize reading readiness, a check list of thirty-three child development items suggested by the teachers as characteristics of this stage was prepared by J. M. Morris. The teachers were asked to use this as a means of recording their observations of pupils' readiness. The teacher ticked the items relevant to the stage reached by each pupil in the 1954 age group.

On the same form, the teachers were asked to predict the standard ('good', 'average', or 'difficulty with reading') which each pupil would reach by the age of 7+ years—that is, the end of their infant schooling. These estimates were completed during the pupils' first and second year of schooling (middle of Autumn term).

In 1959, 169 teachers in 76 schools completed estimates; during 1960, 120 teachers in 64 schools estimated the reading readiness of more than three thousand pupils.

READING READINESS ESTIMATE

SCHOOL CODE...

NAME

Estimates of child's development

A. Makes effort and is eager to learn   ..   ..

Interested in class environment and activities ..

Appendix B

SCHOOL CODE...

NAME

Estimates of child's development

B. Interested in all kinds of books   .. ..

Keen to read   ..   ..

Interested in printed word generally ..   ..

Interested in pre-reading activities and materials

Interested in stories from books   ..   ..

C. Tries and is eager to write   ..   ..   ..

D. Emotionally secure and able to concentrate ..

Rich background of experience and information

Socially co-operative and adjusted to school routine   ..   ..

Physically healthy   ..   ..

E. Sufficient ability to tackle work confidently ..

Good powers of observation and range of ideas

Can think clearly and independently ..   ..

Learns quickly and has good memory   ..

Capable of understanding own and others' mistakes ..   ..

117

School Code..

NAME

Estimates of child's development

F. Can discriminate shapes of letters and words ..

Knows letter names .. ..

Can make auditory discrimination .. ..

Knows letter sounds .. ..

Can discriminate shapes generally .. ..

Recognizes captions to pictures and objects ..

Associates pattern of words with pictures and ideas .. ..

Is aware of left-to-right sequence .. ..

G. Recognizes classroom words generally ..

Recognizes words out of context .. ..

Recognizes words from introductory reader..

Recognizes own name. .. ..

H. Uses reading apparatus correctly .. ..

Handles books carefully .. .. ..

118

	NAME									
SCHOOL CODE...										
Estimates of child's development										

I. Good or adequate oral vocabulary										
Fluent, clear speech										

Total									
Group									

PRE-DICTION	Will become a good reader (at 7+)									
	Will become an average reader (at 7+)									
	Will find difficulty with reading (at 7+)									

Signed...(class teacher)

Date...1959

6. *Primer Criterion* (J. M. Morris)

This method of assessing pupils' reading standards had been used by J. M. Morris (1959) in the Kent investigation, and reported as a satisfactory way of assessing levels of reading achievement in functional terms. The teachers were asked to indicate the 'book level' for each child; that is, the book they were reading in the primer scheme used in the school.

On the same form, the teachers were asked to estimate the reading progress made by each child, using a three-point scale—'good', 'average' and 'slow'. These assessments, like those of pupils' reading readiness, were made during the pupils' first and second years of schooling, the *Primer Criterion* being completed during the Summer term of each year.

In 1960, at the end of the first year's schooling, 147 teachers in 72 schools completed assessments for the 1954 age-group children. At the end of the second year (1961), 135 teachers in 63 schools completed assessments.

PRIMER CRITERION

	NAME						
SCHOOL CODE							
SCHOOL NAME							
BASIC READING SCHEME							
....							
READING STANDARD							
Beyond basic reading scheme							
Book 4							
Book 3							
Book 2							
Book 1 and Introductory Book							
Pre-reading activities only							
Reading progress good							
Reading progress average							
Reading progress slow							

Signed ....(class teacher)

Date ....(1960)

120

Additional Information, Chapter II

Objective measures of pupils' reading attainment

The standardized group test used was the NFER's National Survey 7+ Reading Attainment Test[1], which had been designed for use in the 1960 Survey of first-year junior children. The mean score for the representative sample of 2,733 children from schools in England was 15·24, with a standard deviation of 9·07. The Survey children were aged between 7 yrs. 2 ms. and 8 yrs. 2 ms., with a mean age of 7 yrs. 7 ms. The children in the London schools took the test when they were aged approximately 2 years and 1 year younger than the Survey children. At the end of the infant course, the 3,122 London pupils obtained a mean score of 11·00, with a standard deviation of 8·59.

The test consists of an eight-page booklet containing 30 items of the sentence completion type. The children were instructed to ring the word or words which would complete the sentence. The early items were printed in large script, similar to that used in introductory readers and on flash cards. The first 22 items were composed of progressively more difficult phonic and non-phonic items based on a basic vocabulary of words common to the three reading series, 'Janet and John', 'Happy Venture' and 'Beacon'. The last eight items were of increasing difficulty, both in respect to vocabulary and sentence structure. The reliability co-efficient on 270 cases was ·956 (Kuder-Richardson Formula 20).

Method of calculating school social area. It was decided that the proportional distribution of occupations was the most suitable objective criterion to use as a measure of the school's social environment. Using statistics from the *Registrar-General's Report on Greater London and Five Other Conurbations* (1956), it was possible to calculate a social class index for each school. The Registrar-General's Report provided percentage distributions of the occupations of males for each ward in Greater London, and the social class index for a school was determined by applying appropriate

---

[1] Reading Test: Form N.S.45 by E. J. Standish (NFER, unpublished).

TABLE C/I: *Numbers of Schools, Teachers and Children completing the Various Instruments from the Reading Inquiry which were used in the Study of Teachers' Attitudes*

1. *Attitudes towards and Opinions about Pupils' Home Background*

PART OF THE MAJOR PROJECT	SCHOOLS	TEACHERS	CHILDREN†	
			No.	*Age Group*
1959 Initial Questionnaire	100	198	—	—
Home Background (General) Form 1960	61	275	Children in General	
Home Background (Individual) Form 1961	64	163	3,250	5-6 years
Personal Questionnaire 1960-61	34	148	—	—

2. *Pupils' Reading Attainment and Progress*

PART OF THE MAJOR PROJECT	SCHOOLS	TEACHERS	CHILDREN†	
			No.	*Age Group*
Reading Readiness 1959	76	169	3,944	5+
Estimates 1960	64	126	3,335	6+
Primer Criterion 1960	72	147	3,722	5+
(Book Level) 1961	63	135	3,199	6+
Progress Estimate 1960	72	147	3,674	5+
1961	63	135	3,059	6+
Prediction of 1959	76	168	3,896	5+
Success 1960	64	132	3,219	6+
Group Test of 1960	74	—	3,490	5+
Reading Attainment 1961	65	—	3,122	6+

† Number of children with information, pupils with no information excluded.

weights to the percentage distribution of male occupations for the ward in which the particular school was situated. Thus, an example of the method of calculation would be as follows:

REGISTRAR-GENERAL'S OCCUPATION GROUPING		SCORE	% DISTRIBUTION FOR SCHOOL A
I	(Professional, Managerial, etc.)	3	5
II & III	(Intermediate and Skilled)	2	50

122

IV & V   (Semi-skilled and   1   45
    Unskilled)

Social Class Index for School A= $3\times5+2\times50+1\times45=160$

It was possible to group the schools into nine different social groupings of varying values demonstrating the predominance of higher or lower social classes in a particular area (the ward). It can be seen from Table C/II that it is then possible to group these values into three broad social groupings which correspond fairly closely to the London Conurbation areas, described in the Registrar-General's Report as major areas or divisions of development proceeding from a mainly administrative and commercial centre through broad belts of development of different dates to a fringe area still in process of development; there being within each area further sub-divisions usually based on considerations of geography and homogeneity.

TABLE C/II: *Social Areas and Social Class Indices.*

SOCIAL AREAS	LONDON CONURBATION SUB-DIVISIONS	SOCIAL CLASS INDEX	PERCENTAGE DISTRIBUTION REGISTRAR-GENERAL CLASSES I—V				
			I	*II*	*III*	*IV*	*V*
LOWER WORKING-CLASS	2A	161·2	0·8	7·2	54·4	14·8	24·8
	2B	163·6	1·1	7·9	53·5	13·5	24·0
UPPER WORKING-CLASS	3D	174·0	2·7	11·8	56·8	12·0	16·7
	3C	174·2	2·4	12·6	56·8	11·4	16·8
	3A	176·5	1·8	11·8	61·1	11·5	13·8
MIDDLE CLASS	1	180·7	8·9	17·4	45·5	13·1	15·1
	5D	182·4	4·4	16·2	57·4	9·5	12·5
	5E	188·8	6·4	20·5	55·5	8·5	9·1
	2C	196·6	16·1	22·4	42·0	9·3	10·2

These three areas of different social background on the basis of occupational distribution could be described as follows:

Social Area I: A densely residential area extending on both sides of the city's river, it included mixed industrial and dockside activities. Some of the area had been re-developed since the war when it had been extensively damaged, but parts of the region were still awaiting reconstruction and had all the signs of economic stagnation. Occupations tended to be of the partly-skilled and unskilled nature, and the area could be described as predominantly *Lower Working-Class.*

Social Area II: Having markedly less non-residential property than the previous area, it tended to be a region of residential development rather than an industrial and commercial area. In the middle of the last century a great many of its three-storied villas had been sub-divided and converted into additional housing accommodation. It differed from the previous area in that occupations tended to be predominantly skilled and semi-skilled, although there was a markedly high percentage of employed males in the lowest social class as in the previous area. It was an *Upper Working-Class* area, some of its residents being ambitious to move out of its overcrowded housing conditions to the more truly suburban areas of the outer development of the Authority or into the Home Counties.

Social Area III: This was, in fact, made up of two regions—the outer area of urban development (which was less densely populated than the previous two areas and more suburban in nature) and the much older, central area of the city where residential and non-residential buildings were to be found together. In the latter area, both today and in the past, the older residential property has been taken over for shops and offices. Although these two regions are the outer and inner areas of development, they have similar distributions of occupations, with larger proportions of occupations from the higher social class groups.

In comparison with Social Areas I & II, Social Area III could be described as predominantly *Middle-Class* or at least 'white collar', although in the central area there were one or two 'pockets' of slum housing, so that as a grouping Social Area III tended to be less homogeneous than the other two groupings.

Teachers' social class origin. The data on which this classification was made was available for those teachers who had completed *Personal Questionnaires.* Respondents were asked to supply their father's occupation and that of their mother before and after her marriage. The occupations were classified in two ways: by the Registrar-General's Classification,[1] and by the Hall-Jones Scale.[2]

For the 97 class teachers, the correlation between the two measures of paternal occupation was 0·77. The Registrar-General's grouping was used to code the teachers' fathers' occupations to give a measure of *the teachers' social class origin.*

[1] *General Register Office* (1960). *Classification of Occupations* (1960). London: H.M. Stationery Office.
[2] HALL, J. and CARADOG-JONES, D. (1950). 'The social gradings of occupations', *Brit. J. Sociol.*, vol. I., no. 1.
MOSER, C. A. and HALL, J. R. (1954). 'The social gradings of occupations'. In: GLASS, D. V. ed. *Social Mobility.* London: Routledge & Kegan Paul.

Only the class teachers' social origins were used in the comparison made between the proportions of London women infant teachers in this research and women primary teachers as reported by Floud and Scott (1961) in their study of a selected sample of teachers in grant-earning schools in England and Wales, 1955. Head teachers, some of whom were men, were omitted from the London figures.

TABLE C/III: *Comparison of London 1960-61 and National Survey Figures 1955 of London Infant Women Teachers' and Primary Women Teachers' Social Class Origins*

SOCIAL CLASS ORIGIN		LONDON TEACHERS		†PRIMARY TEACHERS % NATIONAL SURVEY (N=1,449)
		N=96	%	
I	Professional, Managerial and Administrative	13	14	8·8
II	Intermediate	37	39	52·2
III	Manual Skilled	40	41	29·6
IV	Manual Semi-skilled	6	6 ⎫	9·3
V	Manual Unskilled	0	0 ⎭	
		96	100	100

† Based on the Floud and Scott study (1961).

A χ^2 test on these distributions was significant at the 5% level, there being more class I (professional, managerial and administrative occupations), fewer social class II (intermediate), and more social class III (skilled manual occupations) than expected. Floud and Scott showed that the proportion of working-class fathers declines as one moves along what they describe as the line of social hierarchy of schools, whilst that of middle class fathers (major professions, higher administrative and substantial business) increases; also that on the staffs of the primary school (in which infant departments or schools were not differentiated) daughters of skilled manual workers largely predominate over those of professional people of any kind. The difference between the London and national groups is not marked and appears to be in the direction one would expect from the remarks made by Floud and Scott. The distribution of social origins of the London teachers follows the type of pattern which one would expect in relation to teachers employed at the infant stage.

TABLE C/IV: *Distribution of Schools (by Organization and Social Area) and Teachers (by Staff Position and Social Class Origin) completing each part of the Teachers' Attitude Study*

PART OF STUDY	INITIAL QUESTIONNAIRE	HOME BACKGROUND (GENERAL)	HOME BACKGROUND (INDIVIDUAL)	PERSONAL QUESTIONNAIRE	READING READINESS ESTIMATES		PRIMER ESTIMATES		PROGRESS ESTIMATES		PREDICTION ESTIMATES	
	1959	1959	1960	1960-61	1959	1960	1960	1961	1960	1961	1959	1960
SCHOOLS												
Organization												
Infant	53	31	31	19	37	31	34	30	34	29	36	31
J.M. & I.	47	30	33	15	39	33	38	33	38	33	40	33
TOTAL	100	61	64	34	76	64	72	63	72	62	76	64
Social Area												
Lower Working-Class	38	23	24	12	30	24	30	24	30	24	30	24
Upper Working-Class	30	18	20	11	22	20	22	20	22	20	22	20
Middle Class	32	20	20	11	24	20	20	19	20	18	24	20
TOTAL	100	61	64	34	76	64	72	63	72	62	76	64
TEACHERS												
Staff Position												
Head	100	56	—	51	—	—	—	—	—	—	—	—
Class	98	219	163	97	169	126	147	135	147	135	168	132
TOTAL	198	275	163	148	169	126	147	135	147	135	168	132
Social Class Origin	Heads only	Class only	Class only	Class only	Class only	Class only	Class only	Class only	Class only	Class only	Class only	Class only
Middle Class	22	48	29	50	23	24	15	22	15	22	23	24
Working Class	27	43	22	46	15	16	7	17	7	17	15	16
TOTAL	49	91	51	96	38	40	22	39	22	39	38	40

Additional Information, Chapter IV

A. 'GOOD' AND 'POOR' HOMES

Tables D/I and D/II illustrate the teachers' views on the characteristics of 'good' and 'poor' homes respectively, with the items classified into eight categories. Table D/III compares the order of importance of the different categories on the basis of the teachers' answers to the open-ended question in the *Initial Questionnaire*, with that established on the basis of the rating question used in the *Home Background (General) Form.*

Home Background (General) Form

Sub-scores. The *Home Background (General) Form* consisted of 34 items which were divided into eight groups, each of which referred to a specific aspect of the pupil's home background (e.g. motivational, cultural, emotional, etc.), and two additional items relating to general aspects of home background. Each item was scored on a five-point scale, and separate *sub-scores* were calculated for each of these eight groups. The *sub-scores* were the sum of the individual items in each of these eight areas; e.g. sub-score C (motivational items) was arrived at by totalling the five item scores. Tables D/IV and D/V show the means for the sub-scores of teachers in (a) different types of school organization, and in (b) different age groups.

School organization. Sub-scores on 'Parental Interest in School Progress' was the only sub-score area showing significant differences in relation to school organization (5% level of significance). Teachers in junior mixed and infant schools appeared to attach more

TABLE D/1: *Characteristics of a 'Good' Home*

Rank Order All Teachers	Category of Items	Examples of the Items in the Different Groupings	Position of Teacher				School Social Area			Head Teachers (49) Social Class Origin		All Teachers (N 206)	
			Head (N 100)		Class (N 106)		Lower Working (N 79)	Upper Working Class (N 62)	Middle Class (N 65)	Middle Class (N 22)	Working Class (N 27)		
			Total Items (305)	% of Total	Total Items (257)	% of Total	% of Total Items (222)	% of Total Items (163)	% of Total Items (177)	% of Total Items (55)	% of Total Items (70)	Total Items (562)	% of Total
1	MOTIVATIONAL	Parents interested in child's activities, spend time with child, answer questions, parents educated	76	25	75	29	28	26	26	25	23	151	27
2	EMOTIONAL	Stable home life, child loved, family unity, mutual consideration	67	22	64	25	21	24	26	29	24	131	23
3	CULTURAL	'Good' conversation, visits to interesting places, the right amusements, sensible toys	46	15	51	20	17	20	15	18	13	97	17
4	MATERIAL	'Good' food, clothing, adequate sleep, physical provision	31	10	13	5	8	7	8	5	11	44	8
5	MORAL TRAINING	Firm but kindly discipline, moral values, religious faith	21	7	16	6	6	7	7	7	11	37	7
6	REGULARITY, ORGANIZATION, & TRAINING	Regular meals, sleep, habits, cleanliness, Television watching supervised	22	7	10	4	3	7	8	4	7	32	6
7	ECONOMIC	Attractive housing, space to play, mother at home or makes provision, financial security, regular parental employment	20	6	11	4	8	6	3	4	6	31	6
8	INTEREST IN CHILD'S PROGRESS	Parental help with school work, interested in education, co-operate with school	16	5	14	5	6	4	5	7	4	30	5
9	UNCLASSIFIABLE	Quiet, tidy, settled schooling care of toys	6	2	3	1	3	0	1	0	0	9	2

Rank Order All Teachers	Category of Items	Examples of the Items in the Different Groupings	Position of Teacher				School Social Area			Head Teachers (49) Social Class Origin		All Teachers (N 206)	
			Head (N 100)		Class (N 106)		Lower Working (N 79)	Upper Working (N 62)	Middle Class (N 65)	Middle Class (N 22)	Working Class (N 27)		
			Total Items (314)	% of Total	Total Items (295)	% of Total	% of Total Items (252)	% of Total Items (168)	% of Total Items (189)	% of Total Items (57)	% of Total Items (71)	Total Items (609)	% of Total
2	MOTIVATIONAL	Parents not interested in child's activities, questions not answered, parents low intelligence	55	17	70	24	21	20	21	19	17	125	20
1	EMOTIONAL	Insecurity, lack of affection, constant quarrels, bickering, parents divorced, separated, broken homes	72	23	56	19	17	23	24	21	24	128	21
5	CULTURAL	No conversation, poor manners, too much street play, poverty of interests, lack of books	29	9	37	12	13	11	8	14	11	66	11
6	MATERIAL	Poor food, clothing, Insufficient sleep, neglect, lack of physical care	31	10	25	8	12	9	5	7	13	56	9
3	MORAL TRAINING	Laxity, little discipline, children run the streets, lack of faith, indulged	47	15	31	10	12	10	16	14	21	78	13
8	REGULARITY, ORGANIZATION & TRAINING	Irregular meals, sleep, habits, dirtiness, television watching not supervised	17	5	18	6	5	4	8	4	4	35	6
4	ECONOMIC	Overcrowding, financial insecurity, hire purchase, mother working, absent from home	41	13	32	11	13	14	9	16	7	73	12
7	INTEREST IN CHILD'S PROGRESS	No parental interest in schoolwork, education	16	5	20	7	6	7	5	4	3	36	6
9	UNCLASSIFIABLE	Noisy, untidy, broken schooling, etc.	6	2	6	2	2	2	2	2	0	12	2

129

importance to this group of items than teachers in 'infant only' schools (Table D/IV). χ^2 tests on the distribution of sub-scores for different school types were non-significant in all cases.

Teacher's age. Table D/V shows the analysis of sub-scores by age for the smaller group of teachers for whom this information was available. Analysis of variance on each sub-score separately provided no evidence of an age effect. On sub-score E (moral training items) the F-value obtained fell just short of significance at the 5% level.

TABLE D/III: *Characteristics of a 'Good' Home: Comparison of Importance Based on Content Analysis (N=208 teachers) and Rating (N=275 teachers)*

CATEGORY OF ITEMS	RANK ORDER ALL TEACHERS FREE RESPONSE	RANK ORDER ALL TEACHERS RATING ITEMS
Motivational	1	3
Parental interest in school progress	8	8
Cultural	3	6
Moral training	5	2
Organizational (including regularity)	6	5
Emotional	2	1
Economic	7	7
Material	4	4

Since several of the scores showed a tendency for mean score to increase with age, separate t tests between the greatest and least

TABLE D/IV: *Home Background (General) Form: Means for Sub-scores of Teachers in Different School Organizations (N=275 teachers)*

SECTIONS (Basis of Sub-scores)		No. of Items	MEANS FOR TEACHERS IN DIFFERENT SCHOOL ORGANIZATIONS						Range of scores for each section
			Infant only		J.M. & I.		All Schools		
Code	Description		Mean	S.E.	Mean	S.E.	Mean	S.E.	
C	Motivational	5	20·31	0·19	20·88	0·25	20·52	0·15	11-25
A	Parental interest school progress		10·15	0·16	10·69	0·21	10·35	—	04-15
F	Cultural	3	22·07	0·30	22·45	0·40	22·21	0·24	13-30
E	Moral training	6	13·13	0·14	13·26	0·18	13·17	0·11	07-15
D	Organizational	3	12·81	0·16	12·86	0·21	12·83	0·13	06-15
B	Emotional	3	14·35	0·08	14·48	0·10	14·40	0·06	11-15
G	Economic	6	21·88	0·28	21·77	0·36	21·84	0·22	13-30
H	Material	5	21·77	0·20	21·70	0·26	21·75	0·16	12-25
NUMBER OF TEACHERS			175		100		275		

means were applied. Of these, three were significant, sub-score E (moral training) at 1 % and sub-scores B (emotional) and H (material items) at 5 %.

The frequency distributions of sub-scores were bisected (i.e. the total taken above and below the median), and the 2×2 table obtained by taking teachers aged 55+ separately from the others was tested using χ^2. All results were non-significant, and once again sub-score E deviations just failed to reach a significant level.

Total scores. The total of the eight sub-scores was calculated for each teacher, and the mean total score for five groups of teachers classified according to school (a) organization and (b) social area, and teacher's (c) position, (d) social class origin and (e) age. (Table D/VI.) In none of the five groups were overall differences between the means significant nor were the differences between the distribution of total scores. In relation to the age classification, the differences in mean were significant, however, between the youngest group of teachers (those under 25 years) and the oldest (over 55 years)—at the 5 % level of significance, and between the 26-35 years category and the oldest—at the 1 % level.

The *Home Background (General) Form* total score of each teacher was included as one of the variables in (a) the item analysis used to determine the construction of the Attitude to Pupils' Home Background sub-scales, and (b) the analysis of social and psychological factors. On the first analysis, total score correlated at a significant level with several items being tried out for use in the Attitude sub-scales. For instance, high scorers tended to disagree with the statement 'parents should be allowed on school premises at most times of the day', and to believe that 'it would have been better to have lived in another age'. They agreed that hire purchase was more widely used today, but viewed it as a change for the worse. In the second analysis of social and psychological factors, total score correlated significantly with the teacher's age, attitudes to pupils' parents and home background, and authoritarian views (5 % level of significance) but not with the teacher's social class origin and level of anxiety, or the school social area. The tendency was for older, more authoritarian teachers and those with unfavourable attitudes to pupils and their homes, to have higher total scores on the *Home Background (General) Form.*

TABLE D/V: *Home Background (General) Form: Means for the Sub-scores of Teachers in Different Age Groups* (N = 137† teachers)

	SECTIONS (Basis of Sub-scores)		MEAN FOR EACH TEACHER AGE-GROUP					Mean for all teachers	S.E. for Mean of all teachers	Range of scores for each section
Code	Description	Number of Items	Under 25	26-35	36-45	46-55	Over 55			
C	Motivational	5	20·17	20·58	20·40	20·61	21·20	20·53	0·21	11-25
A	Parental Interest in School Progress	3	10·23	10·00	10·37	10·72	11·27	10·46	0·18	04-15
F	Cultural	6	22·37	21·58	22·73	22·44	22·93	22·38	0·33	13-30
E	Moral Training	3	12·60	12·65	12·87	13·44	14·40	13·09	0·15	07-15
D	Organizational	3	12·43	12·12	13·10	12·67	13·33	12·68	0·17	06-15
B	Emotional	3	14·67	14·08	14·43	14·47	14·87	14·47	0·08	11-15
G	Economic	6	21·57	21·81	22·37	21·50	23·80	22·01	0·30	13-30
H	Material	5	21·53	21·12	21·37	21·97	22·47	21·64	0·22	12-24
	NUMBER OF TEACHERS		30	26	30	36	15	137	137	

† Data incomplete for remaining 138 teachers.

133

TABLE D/VI: *Home Background (General) Form: Mean Total Scores for Different Groups of Teachers*

(a)   N=275

VARIABLES	MEANS (for different groups of teachers)
School organization	
Infant only	142·17
J.M. & I.	143·80
School social area	
Lower working-class ..	140·15
Upper working-class ..	144·58
Middle-class	144·29
Teacher's position	
Head teacher	143·88
Class teacher	142·48
All Teachers..	142·76
S.E.	0·87

(b)   N=137   (Data was incomplete for remaining 138 teachers)

VARIABLES	MEANS (for different groups of teachers)
School social area	
Lower working-class ..	140·75
Upper working-class ..	145·10
Middle-class ..	143·79
Age	
Under 25	141·17
26—35	139·12
36—45	143·33
46—55	143·94
55+	150·00
Teacher's social class origin	
1—2	142·54
3—4	143·89
5—6	141·87
7—8	142·56
Teacher's position	
Head Teacher	144·29
Class teacher	142·22
All teachers	142·95
S.E.	1·09

C. INFERENCES ABOUT OCCUPATIONAL LEVELS

Relationship of teachers' estimates of environmental factors to an economic measure. In the *Initial Questionnaire* the heads had been asked to provide estimates of pupils' (a) fathers' occupation expressed as the percentage of paternal occupations in five groups; (b) size of family as the percentage of pupils from different size families; (c) homes with certain possessions—e.g. telephone, garden; (d) mothers working, and (e) families taking holidays outside the British Isles. The last four estimates were on a four-point scale of 'many', 'some', 'few' and 'none'.

An environmental assessment from a less subjective source was available in the form of the J-Index. This Index is an economic measure developed by Gray, Corlett and Jones (1951) and is based upon the percentage of electors liable for jury service within a particular area—the local government unit of the ward. It was possible, therefore, to compare each head's estimates with the J-Index value for the ward in which their school was situated. Using four of the teachers' estimates, it was found that two (homes with telephones and pupils fathers' occupation) correlated significantly with the J-Index scores (1 % level of significance). The relationship between the J-Index and the head's estimates of the percentage of mothers working and of family size was not significant.[1] As was to be expected, since they came from the same source, the four estimates were related, and the association between three of them (families possessing a telephone, mothers working, and pupils' fathers' occupation) was particularly high.   Table D/VII shows the intercorrelations of the four teachers' estimates, the J-Index values, and the teachers' social class origins.

Teachers' general estimates of pupils

Teachers' comments.   Space was provided after each question for the teachers to comment if they so desired.   Their remarks sometimes provided indications of their attitudes towards the particular subject.

Parental interest. The major criticism of the lower working-class area teachers who made comments was that the interest of

---

[1] KEMP (1955) reported that in his study of London pupils' attainment he had used twelve social variables and found that five of them were closely related. The five were: (1) the J-Index, (2) the head's estimate of paternal occupation, (3) Kemp's own estimate of the school's social area, and information from the children in regard to (4) size of family and (5) possession of a telephone.

parents was not sustained and tended to decline after the initial years spent in the primary school when parents had 'satisfied their curiosity'. Several teachers showed some antagonism towards parents; 'the interested ones only want to create a good impression' and 'parents are only willing to listen if the report of a child is good'. However, several commented that interest could be aroused if the

TABLE D/VII: *Intercorrelations of Five Social Variables and Teachers' Social Class Origin*

VARIABLES N=87	J-INDEX SCORES	TEACHERS' ESTIMATES OF				
		Pupils' Fathers' Occupation	*Mothers' Working*	*Homes with Telephones*	*Family Size*	
J-Index scores	1·00	—	—	—	—	
1. Teachers' estimates of pupils' fathers' occupation	+·32**	1·00	—	—	—	
2. Mothers working	N.S. +·13	+·47***	1·00	—	—	
3. Homes with telephones	+·28**	+·67***	+·53***	1·00	—	
4. Family size	N.S. +·07	+·23*	N.S. +·13	+·23*	1·00	

N=45

	J-INDEX	Pupils' Fathers'	Mothers'	Homes	Family	
Teacher's Social Class Origin	N.S. +·13	+·39*	N.S. −·06	+·34*	N.S. −·16	1·00

* = 5% level of significance   ** = 1% level
*** = 0·1% level   N.S. = Not significant

head was able to make personal contact or parents joined the local parent-teacher organization. One teacher believed the interest of both parents was necessary; another excused the lack of interest shown by parents saying that families were large and consequently parents were unable to spare the time.

Fewer teachers in upper working-class area schools commented
and when they did their comments tended to be critical. For
example, they claimed that parents did not set sufficiently high
academic standards for their children, considered 'parents' interest
unnecessary', or that they were 'too ambitious for their children'.
The middle-class area teachers who were critical mentioned the
inability of parents to help their children, to do more than 'merely
inquire about progress', and their concern with 'trivialities'. Also
the latter commented that interest in progress was not confined to
academic progress but that parents implied character development
also. The 'over-anxious' parent was mentioned as having 'as bad
an effect as the disinterested'.

Intellectual ability. Teachers in all three social areas commented
that it was difficult at this age to assess pupils' intellectual ability.
Several teachers in lower working-class area schools suggested that
the apparently below-average standard of intellectual ability of
their pupils was the result of the homes failing to give the children
the necessary vocabulary. Inferior language development often
made it difficult for the teacher to judge the level of individual pupils'
intellectual ability. One teacher made the comment that intellectual
ability could take different forms and added that 'some artistic
intellect could be stamped out by unsympathetic handling'. The
upper working-class area teachers also mentioned the difficulty of
assessing young children, but some added that 'the standard of
intellectual ability applied by the school is high'. The type of
standards applied was also mentioned by middle-class area teachers,
some of whom explained that pupils of average ability were few in
their schools because of the generally low level of parents; the lack
of a 'rich background of experience; the predominance of homes
poor in cultural opportunities'. In the middle-class areas, the
bright child was identified by being 'the one who stands out'.

Quality of home background. The comments of the teachers were
concerned primarily with explaining how they had interpreted the
phrase 'good home background'. There seemed to be a fairly
commonly-held opinion among teachers in lower working-class
schools that most of their pupils were well clothed and fed but that
a 'good' home also implied cultural standards: comments were,
'money is no substitute', 'love and kindly discipline are as necessary
as financial security'. The opinion 'homes of pupils coming to this
school are good in comparison with others in the area' suggested

that some teachers may have had possessive feelings about *their* pupils. The upper working-class area teachers placed less emphasis upon the importance of cultural conditions but tended rather to mention the home's emotional stability. Children might be well fed, well loved but many were considered to have 'too much freedom, the parents indulgent'. Middle-class area teachers also mentioned the importance of discipline and family stability.

Pupils from 'poor' homes: their ability to learn to read. Some teachers qualified their answers by adding such comments as 'if sufficient mental ability', 'if not MD', or 'unless ESN'. Several lower working-class area teachers suggested that the proportion of children able to learn to read depended upon their level of intellectual ability. One teacher remarked that the number of children able to succeed 'depends on innate intelligence and not the home background of the pupil'. Another teacher believed that the degree of success achieved depended upon both the intelligence and the interest of the pupil. However, there was also a group of teachers in these schools who made no mention of the limitations set by intellectual ability and qualified their answers solely in relation to the attitude of the school: 'if the school supplied the encouragement', 'interest', 'stimulation'; 'if the teacher gives the time, patience and encouragement'. These teachers apparently believed that the drive and enthusiasm of the teacher could overcome the lack of motivational interest in a 'poor' home and that their positive attitude would produce success. Several of the teachers in these schools agreed that the process could take longer in the usual circumstances, that progress might be slower especially at the pre-reading stage, and that final standards might be 'mediocre'; as one teacher remarked: 'poor home background often retards but rarely prevents success'. Small classes, individual attention and a variety of methods were mentioned as necessary helpful aids to achieving success with this type of pupil.

Fewer upper working-class area teachers mentioned intellectual ability, and speech defects and hearing difficulties were the limitations mainly referred to in their qualifying comments. What one might term the fatalistic approach to the factor of intelligence appeared again in the statement: 'home background does not mean intelligence; this is determined whether the child reads or not'. These upper working-class area teachers believed also that the process would take longer with their pupils, and specifically mentioned that the skill might not be acquired until the child reached the junior school, the implication being that it was usual for most children to read by the end of the infant school.[1] These teachers expressed the view that success could come 'eventually with the right teaching', implying that the acquisition of the skill by this type of child depended upon the ability and patience of the teacher.

Comments regarding mental deficiency and the process taking longer were made also by the middle-class area teachers, some of whom mentioned that choice of reading material and standards could be related to the home factor. In other words although the proportion of children from 'poor' homes able to learn to read

TABLE D/VIII:

(a) *Intercorrelations of Heads' Over/Under Estimation of Pupils' Social Class and Their Estimates of Pupils' Intelligence and Parental Interest.*

N=40 HEADS	HEADS' OVER/UNDER ESTIMATION	ESTIMATE OF PARENTAL INTEREST	ESTIMATE OF PUPILS' INTELLIGENCE
Over/under estimation	1·00	—	—
Estimate of Parental Interest	N.S. +·25	1·00	—
Estimate of Pupils' Intelligence	+·36**	+·38**	1·00

(b) *Intercorrelations of Heads' Social Class Origin and Estimates of Pupils' Intelligence and Parental Interest.*

N=33 HEADS	HEADS' SOCIAL CLASS ORIGIN	ESTIMATE OF PARENTAL INTEREST	ESTIMATE OF PUPILS' INTELLIGENCE
Heads' social class origin	1·00	N.S. −·16	N.S. +·13

Level of significance: *=5%, **=1%, ***=0·1%
N.S.=Not significant.

[1] One of the findings of the Kent Inquiry (Morris, 1959) was that 54 per cent of first year juniors were at the level of Book 4 and above; that is, only about half the children at the time of transfer were near to completing their reading scheme.

might be fairly high, the type of reading matter chosen and the use to which the skill would be put were closely related to the quality of the home. This attitude, that the teacher can instruct but not inculcate standards of taste, is implicit in the following statement:

> 'I have not found poor home background a hindrance to initial reading, but it shows in deprived imagination and expression at a later stage.'
>
> (Teacher of middle-class origin, middle-class area school.)

General estimates and over/under estimation of pupils' social class

Table D/VIII shows the inter-correlations between the heads' estimates of pupils' intelligence and parental interest, and their social class origins and tendency to over- or under-estimate pupils' social class.

Additional Information, Chapter V

(a)   Estimates of individual children's home circumstances
Substantial numbers of teachers did not answer some of these items, and it was therefore necessary to analyse the differences between school organizations and school social areas from two points of view. These were: (a) the analysis of differences in the proportions of teachers giving definite affirmative or definite negative answers (level of response) and (b) the analysis of differences between the proportions of affirmative responses when only teachers who made definite responses are considered.

School organization differences. The percentages of actual responses to the possible total number of responses for each item for each type of school are given in columns 2 and 3 of Table V/A in the main text (page 49).   Tests showed that these percentages were significantly different only in the case of items 3, 4, 9 and 10 (well ordered routine, stable home, supervised television and parental interest in child's activities), and that more teachers in infants schools did not make any ratings for these four items.   The difference was highly significant for each item.

The affirmative answers for each item were expressed as a percentage of the total number of answers for that item, and this calculation was done separately for the teachers in the two types of school (columns 8 and 9, Table V/A, page 49).   It was found generally that more infant school teachers than junior mixed and infant teachers gave affirmative answers: for items 4, 7 and 9 (stable home, satisfactory housing, supervised television) this difference was highly significant; for items 2, 3 and 5 (familiar with reading, well ordered routine, mother not working) the difference was significant but less so; and for items 1, 6, 8 and 10 (parental help with school work, enough sleep, parental interest in school progress, and parental interest in child's activities) the difference was non-significant.

School social area differences. There was a very significant association between the teachers' ratings of home background and social area on all items.   It was clear that level of response was associated with social area. Teachers in the upper working-class areas were more reluctant to rate their pupils on all items. Also, there was a tendency for rather more teachers in lower working-class areas to make assessments than those in middle-class area schools.

It was thought at first that this result might be due to one deviant school (a Roman Catholic infant only school with 62 pupils in the appropriate age group), but there were also schools in lower working-class areas (an infant only, and a junior mixed and infant—both non-denominational schools with 87 pupils) and in middle-class areas (a junior mixed and infant, non-denominational city school with 34 pupils) which displayed similar but less marked tendencies.

From the teachers who were able to complete this type of assessment, a consistent pattern emerged. The chi-square tests for association between the percentages given in columns 10, 11 and 12 of Table V/A (page 49), indicated that on all items, significantly fewer affirmative answers were given by teachers in lower working-class area schools, whilst teachers in middle-class areas tended to make more positive ratings. This pattern was significant on items 2, 5 and 10 (familiar with reading, mother not working, parental interest in child's activities), and highly significant on the remaining items.

Organization differences within social areas. An analysis of organization within social areas was carried out, and generally the differences between organizations were consistent within areas, but in relation to making responses, differences were less marked in lower working-class areas and less consistent in the middle-class group (Table E/1).

There are several points of considerable interest. Firstly, although generally teachers in the extreme social areas were more willing to complete these types of assessments, it was the teachers in the infant only schools in the upper working-class areas who tended to be less aware of the home background factor. Where they did assess pupils, they tended to be more critical of pupils' home conditions than their colleagues in the combined department schools. Looking simply at the items referring to parental interest, one notices that in regard to parental interest in the school's efforts (items 1 and 8) there are no significant differences in relation to organization in the extreme areas, but in the upper working-class area schools, more teachers in infant only schools are critical. Item 10 deals with parental interest in more general terms, and more teachers in infant only schools had difficulty in assessing pupils as regards this aspect of their homes. Among those completing estimates in the upper working-class areas, more infant only teachers were critical; whereas

in middle-class area schools, it was the teachers in the combined
department schools who returned more negative answers. Then,
of those teachers able to complete assessments in the extreme social
areas, it was the junior mixed and infant teachers who tended to
be less critical of home conditions generally. It is worth noting
that for the item about supervised television (the item for which one
would expect more 'no information' answers), it was the teachers in
the junior mixed and infant schools who were least reluctant to
answer; and when they did, their replies tended to be more critical
than those of teachers in infant only schools. Among the teachers
in upper working-class areas, there was no significant difference
between teachers in the two types of school in regard to level of
response, and a barely significant difference in relation to the type
of answer recorded.

TABLE E/I: *Organization Differences within Social Areas for Teachers'
Estimates of Individual Pupils' Home Background*

Item	Comparison of Levels of Response			Comparison of Affirmative/Negative Answers		
	Lower Working-Class	Upper Working-Class	Middle Class	Lower Working-Class	Upper Working-Class	Middle Class
Parental help with school work	NS	NS	NS	NS	J***	I*
Child familiar with and appreciative of reading	NS	J**	I*	I***	J**	NS
Home with well ordered routine	NS	J***	J**	I***	J***	I**
Emotionally stable home	J*	J**	NS	I***	J**	I**
Mother not working, or if she does, makes provision	NS	J***	I**	I***	J**	NS
Child seems to get enough sleep	NS	NS	NS	NS	NS	NS
Satisfactory housing conditions	J*	NS	NS	I***	J**	I***
Parental interest in child's school progress	NS	NS	NS	NS	J**	NS
Child's television watching planned, supervised	J***	NS	J***	I***	J*	I***
Parents take an interest in child's activities	J*	J*	J**	NS	J**	I**

ere I*** signifies difference with more positive ratings in I schools signicant at 0·1%
 J* signifies difference with more positive rating in JMI schools significant at 5%

TABLE E/II: *Teachers' Estimates of Individual Pupils in Relation to Six Factors Relevant to Pupils' Reading Achievement*

FACTOR		CHILD'S ABSENCE THREE POINT SCALE		CHILD'S LIKING OF SCHOOL THREE POINT SCALE		QUALITY OF CHILD'S HOME GOOD/POOR/NO INFORMATION (Percentage)			CHILD'S INTELLECTUAL ABILITY THREE POINT SCALE		UNDER/OVER ACHIEVEMENT THREE POINT SCALE		PARENTAL INTEREST THREE POINT SCALE	
SCHOOL VARIABLES		Mean	S.E.	Mean	S.E.	Good	Poor	No inform.	Mean	S.E.	Mean	S.E.	Mean	S.E.
SOCIAL AREA	Lower Working-Class	2·49	·02	1·43	·02	64·24	21·36	14·40	2·07	·02	2·03	·02	2·05	·02
	Upper Working-Class	2·46	·02	1·50	·02	63·53	15·76	20·71	2·08	·02	2·03	·02	1·96	·02
	Middle-Class	2·46	·02	1·47	·02	70·96	12·78	16·26	2·04	·02	2·07	·02	1·90	·02
ORGANI-ZATION	Infant Only	2·50	·02	1·44	·01	65·10	15·82	19·08	2·06	·01	2·05	·01	2·00	·02
	J.M. & I.	2·44	·02	1·50	·02	67·44	19·12	13·44	2·08	·02	2·03	·02	1·94	·02
TOTAL		2·47	·01	1·46	·01	65·95	17·02	17·03	2·06	·01	2·04	·01	1·98	·01
Number of Pupils		3,193		3,193		3,184			3,192		3,179		3,158	

144

Appendix E

(*c*)   *Estimates of factors relevant to pupils' reading achievement*

Table E/II shows the mean indices for each of six factors considered relevant to pupils' reading attainment and progress, in relation to the total group and to school organization and social area.

(*d*)   *Estimates of pupils' reading readiness and progress*

Reading readiness. The teachers' estimates covered four areas: pupils' attitudes to reading activities, their intellectual abilities, the development of their perceptual abilities, and the development of their word recognition skills. The school organization and social area differences were as follows:

Organization differences. There were no statistically significant differences between the groups in relation to pupils' *attitudes to reading* activities, but significantly more pupils in infant only schools were reported as being able to tackle work confidently and to understand their own and others' mistakes in respect to *intellectual abilities*.

X However, in regard to the first stage *perceptual abilities* (i.e. discrimination of shapes, letters, sounds, association of symbol and meaning), significantly more pupils in the junior mixed and infant schools were reported as knowing the letter names and their sounds, and as capable of making auditory discriminations, and visual discriminations of shapes. At the second stage of perceptual development (*word recognition skills*) more pupils in infant only schools recognized classroom words and their own names, whilst more pupils in junior mixed and infant schools were able to recognize words out of context.

The second year results showed a marked difference between the groups in relation to *attitude*, more infant only children being described as keen to read and interested in pre-reading activities and stories. Regarding *intellectual abilities*, more junior mixed and infant children were said to learn quickly, and once again more infant only children were described as capable of understanding their own mistakes. In the second year of schooling, the junior mixed and infant pupils still maintained their marked superiority regarding knowledge of the letter sounds, but on the other seven items in this area of readiness the infant only children were markedly superior. Similarly in regard to *word recognition*, significantly more pupils in infant only schools were described as capable of recognizing words from the introductory reader and familiar words in and out of context.

F

Social area differences. During the first year, significantly more pupils in upper than lower working-class areas were reported as eager to learn to read, interested in the printed word and in pre-reading activities and materials. Also, in comparison with pupils in middle-class areas, more pupils in upper working-class areas were reported as being interested in the printed word and in pre-reading activities. When the extreme areas were compared, significantly more middle-class area pupils were described as interested in pre-reading activities and stories from books. The absence of differences in pupils' *attitudes to reading* would seem to reflect the teachers' confidence in their own ability to inculcate this in their pupils. However, it may also have been related to the diverging standards adopted by the teachers.

By the second year, the picture reported by the teachers had changed considerably. The position between the pupils in lower working- and upper working-class area schools was reversed—with significantly more of the former being reported as interested in all kinds of books, pre-reading activities, stories and the printed word generally. Probably the teachers of pupils in the lower working-class area schools believed that they themselves helped considerably in arousing this marked interest, since this had not been apparent when the first estimates were made (i.e. six weeks after pupils started their schooling). In comparison with the upper working-class group, the middle-class group had regained their expected superiority, with more middle-class area pupils reported as interested in the printed word and pre-reading activities; but when the extreme areas were compared, the only significant difference was in relation to interest in stories, and this was in favour of lower working-class area pupils. It is possible that the teachers in the lowest area were over-emphasizing the interest they observed in their pupils; or the difference may have been a real one. The pupils in lower working-class area schools may have gained a genuine enthusiasm for a skill which opened new experiences of excitement and imagination to them (i.e. the appeal of stories); whereas the pupils from the higher social areas, acquainted with the function of the written word since an early age, were unable to experience this enthusiasm with quite the same intensity.

In regard to intellectual abilities, more pupils from upper than lower working-class schools were reported, six weeks after they started school, to have good powers of observation and able to understand their own mistakes. Their powers of observation were, moreover, singled out in comparison with pupils from middle-class area

146

schools. However, more middle-class than lower working-class area pupils were said to learn from their own mistakes. It is interesting that there were no significant differences in the teachers' estimates regarding their pupils' ability to tackle work confidently, to think clearly and independently, to learn quickly, and to have a good memory. By the second year there were no significant differences between the two working-class area groups, and the only significant difference between the three groups was that regarding pupils' ability to understand and benefit from their own mistakes— pupils in middle-class area schools being superior.

Very significant differences existed in favour of the upper working-class area pupils in relation to all the first stage *perceptual ability* items, with the single exception of letter sounds. The proportion of children with this knowledge was lower in the middle-class area than in either of the two working-class areas in which the proportions of children who knew the letter sounds were similar. In comparison with pupils from middle-class area schools, significantly more pupils from upper working-class area schools knew the letter names and sounds, associated patterns of words with their meaning, recognized captions, and made successful auditory discriminations. When the extreme groups were compared, the pupils from the highest social area schools were markedly superior in regard to visual and auditory discrimination, and awareness of left-to-right sequence. The last difference was to be expected since the middle-class children would probably have had more experience with books and reading material. There was no difference, however, between the extreme areas regarding the reported incidence of children knowing the names of the letters, recognizing captions, and understanding symbol and meaning relationships.

By the beginning of the second year of schooling the marked superiority of the pupils in upper working-class area schools had virtually disappeared except in relation to knowledge of letter names. At that stage pupils in middle-class area schools were showing marked superiority on most of the items in this area of reading readiness.

Summarizing the findings in regard to *perceptual abilities*, pupils in upper working-class area schools showed a marked superiority in the first year, which might be explained in terms of the type of teaching they received; on the other hand, it may reflect the tendency of teachers to expect a lower standard from pupils in lower working-class area schools. The pupils in middle-class area schools established their expected superiority in the basic contributory skills (visual and auditory discrimination and word conceptualization) but not in relation to knowledge of letter names and letter sounds, which is probably dependent upon the individual teacher's choice of method and reading scheme.

In respect to *word recognition skills*, pupils in upper working-class area schools were better at recognizing words out of context and their own names than pupils in lower working-class schools. They were also better than the middle-class area pupils at recognizing classroom words. More pupils in middle-class area schools were able to recognize their own names when they started school, and in comparison with pupils in lower working-class areas, were more likely to recognize words out of context. At that stage of pupils' schooling, the groups of pupils did not differ significantly in regard to knowledge of words from the introductory reader. By the second year, there were no significant differences between the two working-class groups, but more pupils in the middle-class area schools were able to recognize classroom words in comparison with pupils from upper working-class areas, and showed a slight superiority regarding knowledge of the introductory reader's vocabulary, compared to the lower working-class area pupils.

The main difficulty in interpreting these findings is that teachers' estimates do not indicate the extent to which:

(a) the differences between pupils from different social areas reflect real differences in the abilities of these pupils;

(b) the differences reflect differences in teaching practice. Pupils may or may not be given the opportunity to demonstrate particular reading readiness characteristics, or they may have received specific instruction and training at school aimed at developing certain reading readiness characteristics. The provision of such opportunities and the method of instruction chosen may be related to the teacher's expectations about pupils from different social areas.

(c) The differences reflect the different standards adopted by teachers in judging pupils from different social areas.

Reading progress

Primer criterion. The class teachers were asked to assess pupils on a five point scale related to the reading scheme used in the school: 0=pre-reading activities; 1=book 1 and below; 2=book 2; 3=book 3; 4=book 4; 5=beyond the basic scheme. Estimates were recorded at the end of the first and second year of infant schooling. Table E/III shows the mean book levels for the different groups, by school organization and social area.

TABLE E/III: *Pupils' Achieved Book Levels* (*six point scale*)

SCHOOL VARIABLES		FIRST YEAR		SECOND YEAR	
		Index	*N.*	*Index*	*N.*
SOCIAL AREA	Lower Working-Class	1·35	1,580	2·97	1,225
	Upper Working-Class	1·52	1,182	3·14	1,057
	Middle-Class	1·53	960	3·20	917
ORGANIZATION	Infant Only	1·42	2,322	3·10	2,013
	J.M. & I.	1·51	1,400	3·08	1,186
	TOTAL	1·45	3,722	3·09	3,199

Progress estimate. The class teachers were asked to assess each pupil's reading progress on a three point scale when they completed the primer criterion estimates. They had to say whether they considered a pupil had made progress during the past year, using the ratings: 1=good; 2=average; 3=slow. Table E/IV shows the mean progress estimate for the different groups.

TABLE E/IV: *Pupils' Reading Progress* (*three point scale*)

SCHOOL VARIABLES		FIRST YEAR		SECOND YEAR	
		Index	*N.*	*Index*	*N.*
SOCIAL AREA	Lower Working-Class	2·13	1,552	1·99	1,204
	Upper Working-Class	2·06	1,171	1·92	1,007
	Middle-Class	2·11	951	1·92	848
ORGANIZATION	Infant Only	2·11	2,294	1·96	1,904
	J.M. & I.	2·10	1,380	1·92	1,155
	TOTAL	2·10	3,674	1·95	3,059

Prediction of success. The class teachers were asked on the reading readiness estimate forms to make a prediction as to the type of reader the pupil would become by the age of seven, i.e. by the time of transfer or completion of infant schooling. Predictions were made six weeks after the children began school, and then a year later, half way through the first term of their second school year. Teachers were asked to classify each pupil as: 1=a good reader; 2=average; 3=would have difficulty with reading. Table E/V shows the mean prediction score for the different groups.

TABLE E/V: *Predictions of Pupils' Success (three point scale)*

SCHOOL VARIABLES		FIRST YEAR		SECOND YEAR	
		Index	*N.*	*Index*	*N.*
SOCIAL AREA	Lower Working-Class	1·93	1,565	1·89	1,208
	Upper Working-Class	1·87	1,148	1·82	1,091
	Middle-Class	1·90	1,183	1·82	920
ORGANIZATION	Infant Only	1·88	2,450	1·86	2,063
	J.M. & I.	1·95	1,446	1·83	1,156
	TOTAL	1·91	3,896	1·85	3,219

Additional Information, Chapter VI

(A). INFANT TEACHER'S PERSONAL INFORMATION

Tables F/I, F/II, F/III, F/IV and F/V show the number of teachers in each category for the school and teacher variables in regard to the factors of teacher's age, marital status, place of birth, length of teaching service, and length of service in present post.

TABLE F/I: *Age Distribution of Total and Groups of Teachers*

AGE GROUP-INGS	TOTAL TEA-CHERS	POSITION		SOCIAL AREA (Class) Teachers)		ORGANIZA-TION		SOCIAL AREA			
								Lower Working-Class		The Rest	
		Head	Class	Lower Working-Class	The Rest	Infant	J. M. & I.	Social Cl. Origin			
								MC	WC	MC	WC
Less than 25 yrs.	32	0	32	16	16	15	17	11	5	10	6
26-35 yrs.	29	2	27	10	17	10	17	3	7	7	10
36-45 yrs.	33	16	17	10	7	9	8	3	7	3	4
46-55 yrs.	38	25	13	3	10	7	6	1	2	6	3
More than 55 yrs.	16	8	8	1	7	4	4	1	0	5	2
TOTAL	148	51	97	40	57	45	52	19	21	31	25

TABLE F/II: *Marital Status Distribution for Total and Groups of Teachers*

GROUP-INGS	TOTAL TEA-CHERS	POSITION		SOCIAL AREA (Class Teachers)		ORGANIZA-TION		SOCIAL AREA			
								Lower Working-Class		The Rest	
		Head	Class	Lower Working-Class	The Rest	Infant	J.M. & I.	Social Cl. Origin			
								MC	WC	MC	WC
Married	48	17	31	14	17	14	17	6	8	10	6
Widowed Separated Divorced }	}17	7	10	5	5	4	6	2	3	3	2
Single	83	27	56	21	35	27	29	11	10	18	17
TOTAL	148	51	97	40	57	45	52	19	21	31	25

TABLE F/III: *Place of Birth for Total and Groups of Teachers*

GROUP-INGS	TOTAL TEA-CHERS	POSITION		SOCIAL AREA (Class Teachers)		ORGANIZA-TION		SOCIAL AREA			
								Lower Working-Class		The Rest	
		Head	Class	Lower Working-Class	The Rest	Infant	J.M. & I.	Social Cl. Origin			
								MC	WC	MC	WC
London	68	29	39	19	20	19	20	6	13	9	10
Provinces	71	21	50	20	30	25	25	12	8	17	13
Dominions and others	9	1	8	1	7	1	7	1	0	5	2
TOTAL	148	51	97	40	57	45	52	19	21	31	25

Appendix F

TABLE F/IV: *Length of Teaching Service for Total and Groups of Teachers*

GROUP-INGS	TOTAL TEACHERS	POSITION		SOCIAL AREA (Class Teachers)		ORAGNIZA-TION		SOCIAL AREA			
								Lower Working-Class		The Rest	
		Head	Class	Lower Working-Class	The Rest	Infant	J.M. & I.	Social Cl. Origin			
								MC	WC	MC	WC
0-5 yrs.	38	0	38	19	19	15	23	11	8	12	7
6-10 yrs.	21	0	21	11	10	9	12	5	6	4	6
11-20 yrs.	43	19	24	6	18	13	11	2	4	9	9
20+ yrs.	45	31	14	4	10	8	6	1	3	6	3
TOTAL	147	50	97	40	57	45	52	19	21	31	25

TABLE F/V: *Length of Service in Present Post for Total and Groups of Teachers*

AGE GROUP-INGS	TOTAL TEACHERS	POSITION		SOCIAL AREA (Class Teachers)		ORGANIZA-TION		SOCIAL AREA			
								Lower Working-Class		The Rest	
		Head	Class	Lower Working-Class	The Rest	Infant	J.M. & I.	Social Cl. Origin			
								MC	WC	MC	WC
Under 3 yrs.	61	7	54	24	30	24	30	14	10	16	14
3-5 yrs.	38	17	21	7	14	10	11	4	3	8	6
6-10 yrs.	32	23	9	5	4	4	5	1	4	2	2
More than 10 yrs.	17	4	13	4	9	7	6	0	4	5	3
TOTAL	148	51	97	40	57	45	52	19	21	31	25

Teachers and their Pupils' Home Background

Infant teachers' self-image. Table F/VI shows the percentage of teachers choosing each of the four personality traits which they considered to be their major strength or weakness in each group of traits.

TABLE F/VI: *Infant Teachers' Strong and Weak Personality Traits*

GROUP	TRAITS	STRENGTH No.	%	WEAKNESS No.	%
A	accuracy	26	19	24	18
	ambition	7	5	71	52
	cheerfulness	80	59	4	3
	decisiveness	23	17	36	27
	TOTAL	136	100	135	100
B	good judgement	10	7	26	20
	sympathy	47	35	13	10
	originality	14	10	76	59
	conscientiousness	64	48	14	11
	TOTAL	135	100	129	100
C	commonsense	90	65	4	3
	enthusiasm	34	25	16	12
	leadership	9	6	49	38
	refinement	5	4	62	47
	TOTAL	138	100	131	100
D	initiative	28	21	26	21
	adaptability	85	64	12	10
	alertness	11	8	28	22
	foresight	10	7	58	47
	TOTAL	134	100	124	100
E	thorough	43	32	30	23
	resourceful	34	25	16	12
	self-confident	12	9	82	62
	truthful	47	34	4	3
	TOTAL	136	100	132	100
F	industrious	41	33	11	8
	systematic	26	21	69	52
	good hearted	50	40	5	4
	cultured	7	6	47	36
	TOTAL	124	100	132	100

N.B. This question was partly based on one reported in the American Study: *Characteristics of Teachers* by David G. Ryans. American Council on Education, 1960.

154

Infant teachers' satisfaction and dissatisfaction with teaching

Table F/VII shows the percentage of teachers selecting each of the seventeen items considered to be either satisfying or dissatisfying aspects of infant teaching.

TABLE F/VII: *Infant Teachers' Satisfactions and Dissatisfactions with Teaching*

ITEM	SATISFYING		DISSATIS-FYING		NO OPINION	
	No.	%	*No.*	%	*No.*	%
1. the social and human value of the job	130	90	1	—	14	10
2. the holidays	115	79	0	—	30	21
3. the opportunity for intellectual growth	46	32	39	27	60	41
4. the environment (general surroundings)	34	24	50	34	61	42
5. one's colleagues	80	55	11	8	54	37
6. the contact with parents	74	51	16	11	55	38
7. the salary	60	41	37	26	48	33
8. the responsibility for others	82	57	7	5	56	38
9. the independence of action	99	68	8	6	38	26
10. the hours of employment	90	62	3	2	52	36
11. the opportunity for self expression	80	55	9	6	56	39
12. the possibility of undertaking out of school voluntary or paid activities of a social service nature	29	20	14	10	102	70
13. the day to day variety of the job	89	61	8	6	48	33
14. the opportunity to work with children	131	90	2	2	12	8
15. the position given to teachers by the community	13	9	70	48	62	43
16. the opportunities for promotion or advancement	12	8	43	30	90	62
17. the opportunity of putting personal ideals into practice	99	68	7	5	39	27

(B) TEACHERS' ATTITUDES TO PUPILS' HOME BACKGROUND

In the light of the findings about infant teachers' self-image and morale, it seemed possible that a teacher's attitude to pupils' home background could find expression in three specific areas: (a) relationships with pupils; (b) relationships with parents; (c) relationships between the school and its social environment. The third area was the most difficult of the three to define, but it seemed to be a basic element in teacher-pupil relationships—involving the teacher's feelings about the school as one social organization among many, e.g. the family, social class groups, the church, etc. The definition of this third area led to consideration of two related aspects— feelings about social change, and optimistic or pessimistic expectations in regard to pupils' aptitudes and abilities.

Six scales in all were constructed: three (sub-scales) as measures of the expression of a teacher's attitudes to pupils' home background, and three as measures of his attitude to social change, general optimism, and authoritarianism.

The items for the sub-scales measuring attitude to pupils' home background were discussed with a group of interested colleagues, teachers and research workers. The items used were selected after an initial try-out with a group of Berkshire teachers. The number of items used in each sub-scale varied, but altogether there were 24 items, and with the authoritarian scale items, they formed question 15 in the *Personal Questionnaire*.

The authoritarian items were adapted from a verion of the 'F' scale used elsewhere in English research.[1]

The first analysis (item selection). In order to select the most discriminating items in each sub-scale, an item analysis was carried out, each item in each sub-scale being correlated with the sub-scale total; the total of the three sub-scales; the authoritarian scale total; and the four variables, teacher's age, social class origin, anxiety measure, and school social area.

The attitude sub-scale items were scored as follows:

    5=strong agreement; 4=agreement; 3=no answer or do not know;

    2=disagreement; 1=strong disagreement with items which were constructed to express or imply favourable attitudes.

The items used in each sub-scale are now given in descending order of discrimination, showing how each item correlated with its subscale total score and with the total attitude score. The items retained in each sub-scale are italicized. After each sub-scale, the aspect of the total attitude which the most discriminating items appear to measure, is discussed.

[1] HIMMELWEIT, H. T. (1955). 'Socio-economic background and personality', *UNESCO International Social Science Bulletin*, vol. 7, no. 1.

Appendix F

SUB-SCALE/AREA EFFECTIVENESS OF THE *SCHOOL*

TYPE OF STATEMENT†	ITEM	CORRELATION WITH SUB-SCALE	CORRELATION WITH TOTAL SCALE
U	9. *The most teachers can hope to do is to ensure that most children enjoy their school days and look back on them with pleasure*	0·61***	0·19
U	8. *The school's function is to teach the basic skills, it cannot influence the way in which such skills are used*	0·56***	0·39***
U	7. *The school is powerless to change standards of taste*	0·56***	0·28**
U	1. One can never change human nature	0·50***	0·17
U	5. Nature is more important than nurture	0·43***	−0·00
F	4. *The school can do much to modify the values a child acquires from home*	0·37***	0·06
F	3. *The school has more opportunities to educate children in the widest sense, than it has ever had before*	0·31**	−0·08
U	2. The money spent on education during the last decade might have been more usefully spent on other social services, e.g. widows' pensions	0·23**	0·14
F	6. The school should be the centre for the intellectual and social development of the community	0·16	−0·15

†U=Unfavourable
F=Favourable

Level of significance:
*=5%; **=1%; ***=0·1%

The most discriminating items in this sub-scale seemed to have in common a feeling about the function of the school, particularly in relation to changing pupils' attitudes and values (which include those to education). This seemed to imply a basic attitude towards pupils' home background, since most of the statements were concerned with the absolute nature of environment. If the teachers were pessimistic about the school's effectiveness, they would be likely to have an unfavourable attitude towards that factor which, they felt, set limitations upon what they could do and hindered them in their teaching tasks.

The items retained were 9, 8, 7, 4 and 3. Items 1 and 5—although correlating highly with the sub-scale total—were considered to be too similar in wording and were worded in unfavourable terms; and favourable items were needed to balance the first three items.

SUB-SCALE/AREA RELATIONSHIPS WITH *PARENTS*

TYPE OF STATEMENT	ITEM	CORRELATION WITH SUB-SCALE	CORRELATION WITH TOTAL SCALE
U	7. *Parents usually cannot see the teacher's side of the problem when something happens at school*	0·61***	0·19
U	5. *Few parents realize that their children are not perfect*	0·58***	0·39***
U	1. *Only too often the home undoes the work of the school*	0·50***	0·22*
F	8. *Parents are usually considerate of teachers' feelings*	0·49***	−0·04
F	9. *Parents usually try to meet the teacher half way*	0·48***	−0·08
F	6. *Parents should be allowed on school premises at most times of the day*	0·43***	0·15
U	3. If parents disagree with the aims of the school, they should take their children elsewhere	0·36***	−0·04
F	2. Most parents make an effort to be friendly with their children	0·31***	−0·17
U	4. The school should make no attempt to justify its aims	0·26**	0·26**

The most highly discriminating items all seemed to have in common, expectations about the sympathy and understanding of parents for the task the school was trying to accomplish, which implied that the home background was such as to value education. The last three items were not retained for various reasons. Item 3 appeared to be related to the teacher's social class origin, more middle class origin teachers agreeing with the statement, whilst item 4 correlated with the teacher's age, the older teacher being more likely to agree with the statement. Item 2 was not included, as sufficient unfavourably-worded items had been used and its correlation with the sub-scale was comparatively low.

SUB-SCALE/AREA RELATIONSHIPS WITH PUPILS AS *CHILDREN*

Type of Statement	Item	Correlation with Sub-Scale	Correlation with Total Scale
F	6. *There are no bad children; there are only bad and unskilled teachers*	0·60***	0·21*
F	3. *All children are fundamentally likeable*	0·59***	0·25*
F	1. *Most children try to do their work to the best of their ability*	0·47***	0·06
F	2. *Few children try to tax the patience of their teachers*	0·45***	−0·08

The difficulty in this sub-scale was to get items worded in unfavourable terms which would differentiate between infant teachers. In the try-outs it was found that teachers tended to show less division of opinion if the statement was worded unfavourably, except in relation to item 5. However, in the item analysis, it was found that this item was associated with age and with the total of sub-scale 1 (effectiveness of the school)—suggesting that this item discriminated between teachers with different educational philosophies probably resulting from their age and training rather than between teachers with different attitudes to children generally. Item 4 was not retained as, although it correlated reasonably well with the sub-scale total, it appeared from discussion with teachers and colleagues that the statement was somewhat ambiguous.

The items retained seemed to distinguish between those teachers who tended to be relatively uncritical of children and those who made qualifying remarks because they considered there were different types of children, by reason of psychological and sociological differences.

Ideally a factor analysis should have been made to test to what extent different factors were operating, particularly that of authoritarianism in relation to individual and groups of items. Re-allocation of particular items to different areas could have been made on the basis of this information. However, an *ad hoc* decision had to be taken regarding the extent of the use of the item analysis. The plan of the research necessitated that items should be selected within the sub-scales, so that the necessary re-marking could be carried out as quickly as possible and provide attitude measures for use in the second analysis.

The scores on each sub-scale were added together to produce a total score which was then used as the measure of each teacher's attitude to pupils' home background.

AUTHORITARIAN SCALE

ITEM	CORRELATION WITH SUB-SCALE TOTAL
3. *Obedience and respect for authority are the most important virtues children should learn at school*	0·78***
1. *Every person should have complete faith in some supernatural power whose decisions he obeys without question*	0·70***
2. *For one to do a good job one needs to know what precisely the person in charge wants to be done and exactly how he thinks it should be done*	0·58***
4. *Children would rather look up to a teacher than treat him as an equal*	0·53***

Despite the comparatively low correlation for item 4, all four items were returned, and the total score used as an indication of authoritarianism.

The second analysis (psychological and sociological factors)

Stage 1. A correlation matrix was constructed covering the following eleven variables:

TABLE F/VIII: *Intercorrelation Matrix for 94 Women Infant Teachers on 11 Variables*

Variable No. and Name	1	2	3	4	5	6	7	8	9	10	11	Interpretation High Score	Low Score
1. School Sub-scale	1·00											Favourable	Unfavourable
2. Parents Sub-scale	+·28**	1·00										Favourable	Unfavourable
3. Children Sub-scale	+·13	+·25**	1·00									Favourable	Unfavourable
4. Total attitude	+·66**	+·81**	+·60**	1·00								Favourable	Unfavourable
5. Authoritarianism	+·24*	+·28**	+·17	+·33**	1·00							Democratic	Authoritarian
6. Anxiety	-·04	-·05	-·04	-·07	-·03	1·00						High	Low
7. Age	-·05	-·05	-·02	-·06	-·23*	-·04	1·00					Old	Young
8. Teachers social origin	-·12	-·05	-·09	-·12	-·05	-·01	-·03	1·00				Upper	Lower
9. School social area	+·12	+·06	-·10	+·05	-·13	-·13	+·14	+·12	1·00			Upper	Lower
10. Political sympathies	+·08	+·12	-·05	+·09	+·33**	-·07	-·22*	+·00	-·08	1·00		Liberal	Conservative
11. Home Background (General) Form	-·15	-·24*	-·10	-·24*	-·20*	+·04	+·21*	-·02	+·11	-·14	1·00	Important	Less Important

Critical values of the correlation coefficient (Single Tail Test)

The political sympathies index was estimated in 7 cases, effective

$N = 94$ 5% value = ·203 (*)   1% value = ·265 (**)

$N = 87$ 5% value = ·211 (*)   1% value = ·275 (**)

Attitude measure
1. Sub-scale 1 (school)
2. Sub-scale 2 (parents)
3. Sub-scale 3 (children)
4. Sub-scale total/attitude to pupils' home background
5. Home background (general) form

Sociological factors
6. Age
7. School social area
8. Social class origin

Psychological factors
9. Authoritarianism[1]
10. Anxiety[1]
11. Political sympathies[2]

[1] The Slater scale was used as the measure of anxiety. This scale comes from the Sutton Booklet (Slater) tests used for the discrimination of neurotic from normal subjects (Bennet, E. 1944). The full scale also covers other aspects but the ten items from the complete *Inventory of Personal Preferences* used were those which were claimed to discriminate among the neurotically anxious.

[2] It was decided not to design a special scale of teacher's social philosophy but a measure of this factor was obtained by using the information from the question on reading habits (Choice of newspaper. See footnote, Chapter VI, page 61).

Findings. Table F/VIII shows the results in detail and the critical values for 5% and 1% or greater levels of significance.

Stage 2. It was not feasible to relate the attitudinal factors in the correlation matrix to all the variables for which information was available from the *Personal Questionnaires.* It was decided that there were four variables from the analysis of the information derived from the *Personal Questionnaires* which would warrant further examination. These were: (a) marital status; (b) place of birth; (c) teaching preferences (type of pupil, form of instruction, and type of lesson planning); (d) status anxiety.[1] The possible relationships between the qualitative variables and the teachers' attitude to home background scale and sub-scales and the authoritarian scale, were examined by categorizing the teachers according to each variable in turn, and then comparing the mean scores for the groups of teachers so formed.

Findings:

Additional variables. No differences in relation to *marital status* or *place of birth* were significant. In regard to the latter variable, the scores of the teachers who were 'provincial' (born in regions outside the London area) were compared with those of the London-born teachers. There was no evidence to support the hypothesis that London-born teachers had more favourable attitudes than provincial teachers.

There were three types of teaching *preference:* type of pupil (bright, slow, varying ability, or of average ability), form of instruction (group or individual teaching), type of lesson planning (day by day or modified plan).

---

[1] Bacchus (1959) had commented on the difficulty of devising a measure of status anxiety, and rather than undertake further scale construction, it was decided that the teachers' reactions to the item concerned with their satisfaction or dissatisfaction with their status in the community (Question 11, Personal Questionnaire) could be used as the measure of this variable. It was possible to divide the teachers into two groups; one group composed of those who had recorded the position given to the teacher by the community as a major dissatisfaction or dissatisfying aspect of their job, and the rest as the other group. Allocation to the first group constituted an indication of status anxiety. This variable was considered because Bacchus had reported an association between it and teachers' attitudes to pupils' abilities in their studies, and had concluded that it was an important factor in pupil-teacher relationships at the secondary school level.

The teachers who preferred bright children were slightly more anxious than those who liked teaching pupils of average ability (5% level of significance). Those who preferred bright children or those of average ability had higher scores on the *Home Background* (*General*) *Form* than those who liked teaching children of varying ability (5% level of significance). Older teachers preferred bright pupils whereas younger teachers seemed to be more interested in the challenge of teaching pupils of varying ability (1% level of significance), and the teachers who preferred pupils of varying ability tended to be less conservative in their political sympathies than those who liked teaching bright or average pupils (5% level of significance).

Scores on the sub-scale attitude to parents and total attitude scale correlated significantly at the 5% level with the type of instruction preferred. Those who preferred group to individual instruction tended to hold more unfavourable attitudes to pupils (5% level of significance). It should be noted that the form of instruction preferred did not correlate significantly with authoritarian views.

Differences in relation to the attitude and personality variables and preferences in regard to the type of lesson planning were not statistically significant.

In regard to the factor of status anxiety, fewer dissatisfied class teachers were found to be in lower working-class than upper working-class area schools (5% level of significance), and dissatisfied heads had less favourable attitudes regarding the effectiveness of the school (5% level of significance).

(C) The Head's Personality and Attitudes

Tables F/IX and F/X show the correlations between the head's personality and attitude to pupils' home background and the four reading attainment variables.

Table F/IX: *Correlations between Head's Authoritarianism and Pupils' Reading Attainment*

Social Area	Group Test 1961	Book Level 1961	Progress 1961	Prediction 1960
Lower Working-Class Schools N=17	+·37	+·15	+·11	−·07
Upper Working-Class Schools N=16	−·27	+·04	−·51*	−·17
Middle-Class Schools N=11	−·12	−·13	+·06	+·44
Total N=47	−·11	−·05	+·13	+·00

N.B. The signs have been adjusted so that a high score on the four reading attainment variables represents good attainment. High scores on the attitude variable indicate less authoritarian attitudes.

Table F/X: *Correlations between Head's Attitude to Pupils' Home Background and Pupils' Reading Attainment*

Social Area	Group Test 1961	Book Level 1961	Progress 1961	Prediction 1960
Lower Working-Class Schools N=17	+·47	+·32	+·34	+·47
Upper Working-Class Schools N=16	+·05	−·04	−·18	+·33
Middle Class Schools N=11	−·21	−·39	−·44	+·29
Total N=47	+·08	−·02	−·00	−·32

N.B. The signs have been adjusted so that a high score on the reading attainment variables represents good attainment. High scores on the attitude variable indicate favourable attitudes.

Bibliography

ADORNO, T. W., FRENKEL-BRUNSWIK, E., LEVINSON, D. J. and SANFORD, R. N. (1950). *The Authoritarian Personality.* New York: Harper; ch. XIV.

ANDERSON, H. B. and BREWER, J. E. (1945-6). 'Studies in teachers' classroom personalities', *Applied Psy. Monographs,* nos. 6, 8, 11.

ASHER, E. J. (1935). 'The inadequacy of current intelligence tests for testing Kentucky mountain children', *J. of Gen. Psy.,* vol. 46.

BACCHUS, M. K. (1959). 'A survey of secondary modern teachers' concepts of their pupils' interests and abilities in relation to their social philosophy and to the social class background of their pupils'. M.A. thesis, University of London.

BARON, G. and TROPP, A. (1961). 'Teachers in England and America'. In: HALSEY, A. H., FLOUD, J. and ANDERSON, C. A. eds. *Education, Economy and Society.* New York: Free Press of Glencoe.

BARR, F. E. (1925). 'A scale for measuring mental ability in vocations and some of its implications'. In: TERMAN, L. M. ed. *Genetic Studies of Genius,* vol. 1, p. 66. Stanford: Stanford University Press.

BAYLEY, N. and JONES, H. E. (Sec. 1937). 'Environmental correlates of mental and motor development: a cumulative study from infancy to six years', *Child Development,* vol. 8, no. 4, p. 336.

BECKHAM, A. S. (1933). 'A study of the intelligence of coloured adolescents of different social-economic status in typical metropolitan areas', *J. Soc. Psy.,* 4, pp. 70-91.

BENNET, E. (1945). 'Some tests for the discrimination of neurotic from normal subjects', *Brit. J. Med. Psychol.,* vol. XX, pt. 3, pp. 271-7.

BERNSTEIN, B. (1958). 'Some sociological determinants of perception: an inquiry into sub-cultural differences', *Brit. J. Sociol.,* vol. IX, no. 2, pp. 159-74.

BERNSTEIN, B. (1960). 'Language and social class', *Brit. J. Sociol.,* vol. XI, no. 3, pp. 271-6.

BERNSTEIN, B. (1961). 'Social class and linguistic development: a theory of social learning'. In: HALSEY, A. H., *et al.* eds. *Education, Economy and Society.* New York: Free Press of Glencoe.

BIRCHMORE, B. (1951). 'A study of the relationship between pupils and teachers in certain classes in a secondary grammar school'. M.A. thesis, University of London.

BOYD, G. (1952). 'The levels of aspiration of White and Negro children in a non-segregated elementary school', *Jour. Soc. Psychol.,* 36.

BURKS, B. S. (1928). 'The relative influence of nature and nurture upon mental development: a comparative study of foster-parent/foster-child resemblance and true-parent/true-child resemblance'. In: *Twenty-Seventh Year Book of the National Society for the Study of Education,* part I. Chicago: Public School Publishing Company.

BURT, C. (1937). *The Backward Child.* (Revised 1961). London: University of London Press.

BURT, C. (1947). 'Selection for secondary schools', *Brit. J. Educ. Psychol.,* vol. XVII, pt. II.

CAMPBELL, F. (1956). *Eleven Plus and All That.* London: Watts.

CHAPIN, F. S. (1928). 'A quantitative scale for rating the home and social environment of middle class families in an urban community', *Jour. of Educ. Psychol.*, vol. XIX, pp. 99-111.

CICOUREL, A. V. and KITSUSE, J. I. (1963). *The Educational Decision-Makers.* New York: Bobbs-Merrill.

CLARK, K. B. (1963). 'Educational stimulation of racially disadvantaged children'. In: PASSOW, A. H. ed. *Education in Depressed Areas.* New York: Bureau of Publications, Teachers College, Columbia University.

CURRY, R. L. (1962). 'The effect of socio-economic status on the scholastic achievement of sixth grade children', *Brit. J. Educ. Psychol.*, vol. XXXII, pt. I, pp. 46-9.

DAVIDSON, H. H. and LANG, G. (1960). 'Children's perceptions of their teachers' feelings toward them related to self perception, school achievement and behaviour', *J. Exp. Educ. Psychol.*, 29:2, pp. 107-18.

DELANEY, M. (1954). 'An investigation into children's dependence on and reactions to a teacher's judgement with regard to their success or failure in school work'. M.A. thesis, University of London.

DOUGLAS, J. W. B. (1964). *The Home and the School.* London: MacGibbon & Kee.

EYSENCK, H. J. (1947). 'Primary social attitudes I. The organization and measurement of social attitudes', *Int. J. Opin. Att. Res. I.*, pp. 49-84.

EYSENCK, H. J. (1953). *Uses and Abuses of Psychology.* Harmondsworth: Penguin; p. 270.

EYSENCK, H. J. (1954). *The Psychology of Politics.* London: Routledge.

EYSENCK, H. J. and CHOWN, S. (1949). 'An experimental study in opinion attitude methodology', *Int. J. Opin. Att. Res.*, 3, pp. 47-86.

FRASER, E. (1959). *Home Environment and the School.* London: University of London Press.

FREEMAN, F. N., HOLZINGER, K. S. and MITCHELL, B. C. (1928). 'The influence of environment on the intelligence, school attainment and conduct of foster children'. In: *Twenty-Seventh Year Book of the National Society for the Study of Education.* Chicago: Public School Publishing Company.

FREEMAN, F. N., HOLZINGER, J. K. and NEWMAN, H. N. (1937). *Twins: a Study of Heredity and Environment.* Chicago: University of Chicago Press.

FLEMING, C. M. (1943). 'Socio-economic level and test performance', *Brit. J. Educ. Psychol.*, vol. XIII, pt. II.

FLOUD, J. (1962). 'The sociology of education'. In: WELFORD, A. T. ed. *Society: Problems and Methods of Study.* London: Routledge; pp. 521-40.

FLOUD, J. and SCOTT, W. (1961). 'Recruitment to teaching in England and Wales'. In: HALSEY, A. H., *et al.* eds. *Education, Economy and Society.* New York: Free Press of Glencoe; p. 540, Table II.

FLOUD, J., HALSEY, A. H. and PARTIN, F. M. (1956). *Social Class and Educational Opportunity.* London: Heinemann.

FURFEY, P. H. (1928). 'The relation between socio-economic status and intelligence of young children as measured by the Linfert-Hierholzer scale', *J. of Gen. Psychol.*, 35, pp. 478-80.

FURFEY, P. H. and MUEHLENBEIN, J. (1932). 'The validity of infant intelligence test', *J. of Gen. Psychol.*, 40, pp. 219-23.

GAW, F. (1925). 'A study of performance tests', *Brit. J. of Psychol.*, vol. XV.

GLASS, R. (1948). *The Social Background of a Plan: A Study of Middlesbrough.* London: Routledge.

GOODACRE, E. J. (1961). 'Teachers and the socio-economic factor', *Educ. Research*, vol. IV, no. 1, pp. 56-61.

GOODACRE, E. J. (1967). *Reading in Infant Classes.* 'Teaching Beginners to Read', Report No. 1. Slough: NFER.

GOODENOUGH, F. (1927). 'The relationship of the intelligence of pre-school children to the education of their parents', *School of Soc.*, 26, pp. 54-6.

GORDON, H. (1923). 'Mental and Scholastic Tests Among Retarded Children: an Inquiry into the Effects of Schooling on the various Tests', Board of Education Pamphlets. London: H.M. Stationery Office.

GOUGH, H. J. (1946). 'The relationship of socio-economic status of personality inventory and achievement test scores', *Jour. of Educ. Psychol.*, vol. XXXVII, pp. 527-40.

GRAY, P. G., CORLETT, T. and JONES, P. (1951). *The Proportion of Jurors as an Index of the Economic Status of a District.* London: Central Office of Information.

HALL, J. and CARADOG-JONES, D. (1950). 'The social grading of occupations', *Brit. J. of Sociol.*, vol. 1, no. 1.

HEBB, D. O. (1949). *The Organization of Behaviour.* New York: Wiley.

HIMMELWEIT, H. T. (1954). 'Social status and secondary education since the 1944 Act: some data for London'. In: GLASS, D. V. ed. *Social Mobility in Britain.* London: Routledge; p. 149.

HIMMELWEIT, H. T. (1955). 'Socio-economic background and personality'. In: UNESCO. *International Social Science Bulletin*, vol. 7, no. 1.

HOLLEY, C. E. (1916). 'The relationship between persistence in school and home conditions', *Fifteenth Year Book of the National Society for the Study of Education.* Chicago: Public School Publishing Co.; pt. II, p. 119.

INGLIS, W. B. (1948). 'The early stages of reading: a review of recent investigations'. In: *Studies in Reading*, vol. 1. London: University of London Press.

JACKSON, B. (1964). *Streaming: an Education System in Miniature.* London: Routledge.

JACKSON, B. and MARSDEN, D. (1962). *Education and the Working Class.* London: Routledge.

JONES, D. C. (1934). 'Social factors in secondary education'. In: *The Social Survey of Merseyside*, vol. 3. London: Hodder & Stoughton; pp. 158-200.

JONES, E. H. (1928). 'A first study of parent-child resemblance in intelligence'. In: *Twenty-Seventh Year Book of the National Society for the Study of Education*, part I, pp. 61-72. Chicago: Public School Publishing Company.

KEMP, L. C. D. (1955). 'Environmental and other characteristics determining attainment in primary schools', *Brit. J. Educ. Psychol.*, vol. XXV, pt. II, 67-77.

KERLINGER, F. N. and KAYA, E. (1959). 'The construction and factor analytic validation of scales to measure attitudes towards education'; and 'The predictive validity of scales constructed to measure attitudes towards education', *Educ. Psychol. Meas.*, 19, pp. 13-29; 305-17.

LEAHY, A. M. (1935). 'Nature-nurture and intelligence', *Genetic Psy. Mono.*, vol. XVII.

LEAHY, A. M. (1936). *Measurement of Urban Home Environment.* Minneapolis: University of Minnesota Press.

LEWIN, K., LIPPITT, R. and WHITE, R. (1939). 'Pattern of aggressive behaviour in experimentally created social climates', *J. of Soc. Psychol.*, vol. 10.

LOEVINGER, J. (1939). 'Intelligence as related to socio-economic factors'. In: *Thirty-Ninth Year Book of the National Society for the Study of Education*, part I, pp. 159-210. Chicago: Public School Publishing Company.

LYNN, R. (1959). 'Environmental conditions affecting intelligence', *Educ. Research.*, vol. 1, no. 3, p. 52.

MACCLEANATHAN, R. H. (1934). 'Teachers and parents study children's behaviour', *J. of Educ. Soc.*, vol. 17.

MCCLELLAND, D., *et al.* (1959). 'Issues in the identification of talent'. In: McClelland, D., *et al. Talent and Society.* New York: Van Nostrand.

MCLAREN, V. M. (1950). 'Socio-economic status and reading ability—a study in infant reading'. In: *Studies in Reading*, vol. II. London: University of London Press; p. 50.

Teachers and their Pupils' Home Background

MAYS, J. B. (1962). *Education and the Urban Child.* Liverpool: Liverpool University Press; pp. 133-50.

MINISTRY OF EDUCATION (1954). *Early Leaving: A Report of the Central Advisory Council for Education (England).* London: H.M. Stationery Office.

MITCHELL, G. (1959). *Sociology. The Study of Social Systems.* University Tutorial Press; p. 146.

MORRIS, J. M. (1959). *Reading in the Primary School.* NFER Publication No. 12. London: Newnes Educational.

MOSER, C. A. and HALL, J. R. (1954). 'The social gradings of occupations'. In: GLASS, D. V. ed. *Social Mobility.* London: Routledge.

NISBET, J. D. (1953). 'Family environment; a direct effect of family size on intelligence', *Occasional Papers on Eugenics,* No. 8. London: Cassell.

OLIVER, R. A. C. and BUTCHER, H. J. (1962). 'Teachers' attitudes to education: the structure of educational attitudes', *Brit. J. Soc. & Clin. Psychol.,* vol. 1, part 1, pp. 56-69.

PASSOW, A. H. ed. (1963). *Education in Depressed Areas.* New York: Columbia University Press.

Registrar General's Classification of Occupations. (1960). London: H.M. Stationery Office.

RUDD, W. G. A. and WISEMAN, S. (1962). 'Sources of dissatisfaction among a group of teachers', *Brit. J. Educ. Psychol.,* vol. XXXII, p. 275.

RYANS, D. G. (1960). *Characteristics of Teachers: their Description, Comparison and Appraisal.* Washington, D.C.: American Council on Education.

SANDON, F. (1961). 'Attendance through the school year', *Educ. Research,* vol. III, no. 2.

SHAW, D. C. (1943). 'The relation of socio-economic status to educational achievement in grades four to eight', *Jour. of Educ. Research,* vol. XXXVII, pp. 197-201.

STOTT, D. H. (1960). 'Interaction of heredity and environment in regard to "measured intelligence" ', *Brit. Jour. Educ. Psychol.,* vol. XXX, pt. 2, pp. 95-102.

TAUSSIG, F. W. (1928). *Principles of Economics.* New York: Macmillan.

VAN ALSTYNE, D. (1929). *The Environment of Three-Year-Old Children: Factors related to Intelligence and Vocabulary Tests.* Teach. Col. Columbia Univ. Contrib. to Educ. no. 366; p. 108.

VERNON, P. E. (1955). 'The assessment of children', *Studies in Education,* no. 4. London: Evans.

WICKMAN, E. K. (1928). *Children's Behaviour and Teacher's Attitude.* The Commonwealth Fund, New York.

WILLIAMS, J. H. (1916). 'The Whittier scale for grading home conditions', *Jour. of Delinquency,* vol. I.

WILSON, A. B. (1963). 'Social stratification and academic achievement'. In: PASSOW, A. H. ed. *Education in Depressed Areas.* New York: Bureau of Publications, Teachers College, Columbia University; p. 232.

Index

Absenteeism
pupils' 17, 35, 36
Achievement
over/under achievement, pupils'
53-4, 144
Age
of teachers 4, 9, 16, 32, 59, 130-4,
151, 161
Aims
of the attitude study xi, xiii
of the project xi
Attitudes
pupils', to learning to read 145-6
teachers', to pupils' home background 21, 67-8, 71-2, 155-63
Educational significance and statistical
significance 14
Estimates of pupils
general 11, 26, 46-7, 135-9
individual xiii, 11, 19, 48-57, 141-50
Head teachers'
personality xiii, 21, 28, 69-72
Home
aspects supporting learning to read
xiii, 15, 27-8, 53-4
background, teachers' attitude to
21, 67-8, 71-2, 155-63
circumstances, individual pupils
48-50, 141
'good', characteristics of
xiii, 16, 28-32, 127-8
'poor', characteristics of
xiii, 16, 28-32, 129
quality of 46, 137
Intellectual ability
pupils' 46, 53, 137
Interest
parental 17, 39, 46, 135-7
Lateness
pupils' 35, 36
Mothers, working 50
Occupation, paternal
of pupils xiii, 18-9, 41-6
Parents
expectations 3
interest, amount of 46
interest, indications of 17, 39, 135-7
parent-teacher co-operation 16, 33
paternal occupation 18, 41-6, 135-6
role of 18
visiting school 33
reasons for 34

Perceptual abilities
pupils' 145, 147-8
Personality
teachers' 4-6, 21, 70
Personality characteristics
pupils' 5, 19, 51-3
Plowden Report iii, xii, 1, 17, 61
Pupils
abilities associated with differences
in home background 15, 27
absenteeism 17, 35
reasons for 17, 36
accompanied to school 34
attitude to learning to read 145-6
clothing 17, 38
from 'poor' homes, ability to learn
to read 46, 138-9
home circumstances
aspects supportive of learning to
read xiii, 15, 27-8, 53-4
'good' home, characteristics of
xiii, 16, 28-30, 127-8
individual pupil 48-50, 141
'poor' home, characteristics of
xiii, 16, 28-30, 129
quality of 46, 138
rating characteristics of the 'good'
home 30-2
intellectual ability 46, 53, 137
lateness 35
reasons for 36
liking for school 19, 53-4
material circumstances 37-8
needy families, pupils from 39
over/under achievement 53-4, 144
paternal occupation, recording
xiii, 44
perceptual abilities 145, 147-8
personality characteristics 5, 19, 51-3
reading attainment
estimated 9, 20, 48, 54-8,
145-50, 164
tested 9, 121, 164
reading, prediction of success
9, 48, 58, 149-50, 164
reading progress 9, 20, 48, 54-8,
145-50, 164
reading readiness 9, 20, 48, 54-8,
145-50, 164
word recognition skills 148
working mothers 50

ng forms 9, 26, 41, 46,

H.B. (Individual) form 9, 48, 100-6
initial questionnaire 9, 26, 79-94
personal questionnaire 9, 58, 106-15
primer criterion 9, 48, 119-20
reading readiness estimate 9, 48, 116-9
Reading
prediction of success 9, 48, 58, 149-50, 164
progress 9, 20, 48, 54-8, 145-50, 164
pupils' attitudes to 145-6
Reading ability
pupils from 'poor' homes 46, 138-40
Reading attainment
estimated 9, 20, 48, 54-8, 145-50, 164
tested 9, 121, 164
Reading readiness 9, 20, 48, 54-8, 145-50, 164
Research
future 73-4
previous 1-8
Role
parents' 18
teachers' 1-3
Sample schools 77-8
School
organization, differences in relation to xiii, 18, 23, 37-8, 40, 51-2, 54, 65-6, 141-50
organization, types of 10-13
religious denomination 9, 32
Selection and representativeness of sample of schools 77-8
Significance, statistical
and educational significance 14
Social area of school
definition 11-2, 123-4
differences in relation to 16, 19-20, 22, 30, 32, 37-8, 40, 46, 51, 53, 65-6, 141-50, 161
importance of 5-6
method of calculation 121-3

Statistical significance
and educational significance 14
Teachers
age 4, 9, 16, 32, 59, 130-4, 151, 161
attitude to pupils' home background 21, 68, 71-2, 155-63
attitudes to money 24
authoritarianism 6, 16, 21, 68, 161
birthplace 59, 162
classification of parents' occupation 18-9, 43-4, 135-6
education, training and experience 60
effectiveness 1, 3-4
head teachers' personality xiii, 21, 28, 69-72
infant teachers xiii, 20, 59
inferences about paternal occupations xiii, 18-9, 40-6
job dissatisfaction 64-6
job satisfaction 21, 64-6
leisure activities 62
length of service 62
marital status 59, 162
neighbourhood of residence 61
personality 4-6, 21, 70
position, differences in relation to xiii, 23-4, 28, 30, 34, 38, 40, 65
preferences in teaching 63, 162-3
reading habits 61
role 1-3
self-image 21
sex 59
sex differences 22, 68
social class origin, differences in relation to xiii, 18, 24, 40-1, 60, 141-50, 161
status anxiety 161-3
time in present post 60
visiting of pupils' homes 16, 35
Visits to school
by parents 33, 34
Word recognition skills 148
Working mothers 50